PRAGUE'S CHURCHES

PRAGER | PRAGUE'S
KIRCHEN | CHURCHES

Ivan Doležal · Jiří Doležal

Jiří Burian

PRAGER KIRCHEN
PRAGUE'S CHURCHES

Mladá fronta

ISBN 80-204-0312-4

EINES der grundlegenden Charakteristika des historischen Prags sind seine Sakralbauten. Die Stadtsilhouette ist fast von jedem Blickwinkel aus mit Vertikalen durchwoben. Von den steilen Türmen der Veitskathedrale hoch über der Stadt, über den Wald gotischer Türme, Türmchen und Glockentürme bis zu den Kuppeln und Kuppeldächern der barocken Kirchenbauten – alle verleihen dem Stadtrelief seinen unverwechselbaren Rhythmus. In der bedrückenden Enge mittelalterlicher Straßen und Gassen bis hin zu den offenen Plätzen breiten sich mit strenger Gewichtigkeit die Fassaden der ausladenden dreischiffigen Pfarrkirchen und Konventklöster aus, die eine Lebensbedingung des mittelalterlichen Prags darstellten. Mit emotivem Nachdruck des Formenreichtums fesseln die Fassaden der Barockkirchen oder der in barocke Stilgewänder gekleideten älteren Bauten den Blick der Vorübergehenden. Und schließlich künden, wenn auch nur wenige gänzlich erhaltene Bauten von der Größe der Stadt in jenen Zeiten, da sich künftiger Ruhm und künftige Größe zu entfalten begannen.

Der vorliegende Band ist ein kurzer Überblick und der Prager Sakralarchitektur gewidmet – ihres kulturellen Wertes wegen und auch deshalb, da sich in ihr das komplizierte Geflecht der Geschehnisse in der Stadt und im Land spiegelt ebenso wie die Veränderungen im Leben der Bewohner, die großen Wendepunkte, Spannungen und Umbrüche von geschichtlicher Bedeutung.

Prag war durch seine zentrale Lage dafür vorbestimmt, zu einem Sitz zentraler Herrschermächte und Zentrum des geistigen Lebens und der Kultur sowie Wirtschaftszentrum des Landes zu werden. Das alles ist ohne die aktive Beteiligung des zahlreichen Klerus, des Bischofs und seines Hofs ebenso der zahlreichen Orden und Priestertümer in allen Prager Städten undenkbar.

Andererseits schufen die Stellung der Herrscher und die wirtschaftliche Prosperität der Stadt Bedingungen für die sich ununterbrochen entwickelnden Bauunternehmen und die steigenden Kulturambitionen, in deren Vordergrund eben die Errichtung und Ausgestaltung von Heiligtümern unterschiedlichster Bestimmung und Funktion standen.

Nicht nur der Bereich der geistigen Führung lag in den Händen des Klerus, er war in den meisten Entwicklungsphasen des böhmischen mittelalterlichen Staates an dessen Verwaltung, an der Leitung der Herrscherkanzleien und Diplomatie beteiligt. Etwa seit dem Jahrtausendende wirkte beim St.-Veits-Kapitel eine lateinische Schule, bis zur Gründung der Universität durch Karl IV. die höchste Lehrstätte im Lande. Bezeichnend ist, daß dessen Kanzler der erste Prager Erzbischof Ernst von Pardubice war.

Der Baueifer der Kirche, von Herrschern und später auch Privatstiftern brachten neue Stilanregungen ins Land, und es war in erster Linie Prag, wo sich die Rezeption und Einbürgerung neuer Stilsysteme und schöpferischer Ideen abspielte. Von hier aus verbreiteten sich die neuen schöpferischen Errungenschaften nach ganz Böhmen und nicht nur einmal bis über dessen Grenzen hinaus.

Die ideelle Welt Europas, verwoben mit dem Netz von Klöstern unterschiedlichster Orden, deren Anzahl unaufhörlich stieg und schrittweise in Böhmen Wurzeln schlug, wurde durch einzelne Mönche oder ins Land kommende Konvente, durch Wallfahrten oder Reisen der böhmischen Fürstenschaft ins Ausland und bald danach regelmäßig durch Ordenskapitele vermittelt. Einen Stimulus stellte auch die Universitätsgründung dar, das allgemein zugängliche Studieren, das es dem begierigen Denken im Verlauf einer Generation ermöglichte, den gedanklichen Kwaß des Jahrhunderts aufzunehmen, ihn klar zu formulieren und zu beeinflussen. Nach dem Westfälischen Frieden wurden die rekatholisierenden Bemühungen der siegreichen

Habsburger bald von der administrativen und repressiven Seite auf die aktive allseitige Propagierung verlagert, die an der Wende des Jahrhunderts in der Explosion des Hochbarocks gipfelte. Das veränderte das Antlitz Prags durch die Errichtung Dutzender neuer Heiligtümer und Klöster sowie umfangreicher und oft radikaler Umbauten mittelalterlicher Objekte.

Die Anzahl der Kirchenbauten – schon zuvor erheblich – wurde angesichts der Stadtbedingungen an der Neige zum 18. Jahrhundert äußerst überzogen. Die Zeit der Reduktion begann, die die Reformen des erlauchten Absolutisten Kaisers Josef II. einleiteten. Vor allem die Klöster waren davon betroffen. Im Verlauf des 19. Jahrhunderts, als sich Prag aus seiner Provinzidylle herauswandt und sich zu einem Zentrum von Industrieunternehmen, des Handels und des erneuerten national-kulturellen und politischen Lebens entwickelte, führte die Destruktion zur Vernichtung meist kleiner Objekte, aber oft von unersetzbarem Wert. Gegen Ende des Jahrhunderts begann man, die Prinzipien des modernen Denkmalsschutzes einzuhalten, die die überwiegende Mehrheit der Prager Kirchendenkmäler nicht nur als Kulturwert bewahrten, sondern auch deren Nachklingen im Kontext historischer Stadträume.

Die Prager Kirchen stellen nicht nur eine steinerne Chronik, Bauschmuckstücke dar, sondern sind gleichzeitig ein unerschöpfliches Schatzkästlein von Werken der Malerei, Bildhauerei, von Mobiliar, Paramenten, lithurgischen Gefäßen, musikalischen und literarischen Denkmälern sowie monumentalen Schöpfungen und kleinen Schmuckstücken.

Heute beleben sie sich wieder als Plätze kirchlicher Versammlungen und persönlicher Kontemplation, sie erfreuen sich aber auch des Interesses jener, die eintreten, um deren Formensprache und historische Botschaft zu bewundern oder den Tönen alter Kompositionen zu lauschen.

Die Entwicklung des frühfeudalen böhmischen Staates war von Beginn an mit der kirchlichen Landesgeschichte verwoben. Der Prozeß der Vereinigung Böhmens unter der Oberherrschaft der Přemyslidenfürsten ging Hand in Hand mit der Christianisierung vonstatten. Dazu kam es kurz nach 880,

als Bořivoj I., Fürst vom Stamme der Tschechen, in Mähren die Taufe vom Bischof des hl. Methodius entgegennahm. Nachdem er sich mit Hilfe Mährens eine feste Regierung geschaffen hatte, errichtete er die ersten christlichen Heiligtümer, zuerst die St.-Klemens-Kirche in seinem Geschlechtersitz Levý Hradec und danach die Marienkirche in Prag – einem Ort von wahrscheinlich vorchristlichen Kult- und Stammesversammlungen, den er usurpierte und die Burgstätte Prag gründete – die Vorgängerin der Prager Burg.

Das gesamte dramatische 10. Jahrhundert hindurch setzten die Přemysliden in der Errichtung des neuen Sitzes fort. Bořivojs Sohn Wratislaw gründete die älteste Kirche des hl. Georg – für die folgenden zwei Jahrhunderte stammesfürstliche Begräbnisstätte. Der Enkel Wenzel errichtete die älteste Kirche, die dem neuen Landespatron geweiht war – St. Veit – die Rotunde an der Stelle der heutigen St.-Veits-Kapelle. Fürst Wenzel bemühte sich wahrscheinlich um eine größere kirchliche Selbständigkeit seines Landes – bislang dem Regensburger Bistum untergeordnet –, gleichermaßen wie er sich von der Unterordnung gegenüber bayerischen Herzögen abwandte und sich mit der sächsischen Dynastie verbündete. Die Machtkämpfe beendeten 935 die Absichten und das Leben von Fürst Wenzel. Er wurde kurz darauf zusammen mit seiner Großmutter Ludmilla heilig gesprochen.

Die Bedeutung Wenzels als Heiliger, als Stammes- und Landespatron, als mystischer Herrscher und Fürsprecher Böhmens, von dem die Fürsten und Könige ihre Macht herleiteten, überschritt weit die Grenze der Zeiten, trotz seiner kurzen irdischen Herr-

Von der Karlsbrücke aus öffnet sich der Blick auf die Konfiguration der barocken Klosterareale der Kreuzherren und des Klementinums. | Charles Bridge affords a fine view of the configuration of the Baroque monastery areas of the Knights of the Cross and the Clementinum.

schaftszeit. Boleslav I., der jüngere Bruder und als
Teilnehmer der Verschwörung büßend, setzte nach
Konsolidierung der Verhältnisse im Land in der
Politik des Bruders fort. Sein Sohn Boleslav II.
erreichte bereits beim päpstlichen Stuhl die Erhöhung
Prags zum Bistum. Die Gesandtschaft nach Rom
wurde durch die Schwester des Fürsten Mlada
geführt, die als Ordensfrau und als erste Kloster-
vorsteherin der Kanonissen bei der St.-Georgs-Kir-
che zurückkehrte. Das zweite Kloster des Benedik-
tinerordens gründete 993 in Břevnov Boleslav II. auf
Anregung von Bischof Adalbert, der bald darauf
Märtyrer und dritter Landesheilige wurde. Zusammen mit dem Bistum entstand bei der St.-Veits-Kir-
che auch das Metropolitenkapitel.

Im 11. Jahrhundert festigte sich der Přemysliden-
staat weiter. Nach der Jahrhundertmitte bemühte sich
Spytihněv II. um die kirchliche Verselbständigung
durch die Errichtung eines Erzbistums für das
böhmische Fürstentum wie es bereits in Ungarn und
Polen war. Deshalb begann er an der Stelle der
Wenzelsrotunde den Bau einer neuen Kirche. In Gestalt einer zweichorigen Basilika errichtete sie sein
Bruder Wratislaw II., der erste böhmische König.
Eine Erzdiözöse blieb allerdings bis Mitte des
14. Jahrhunderts ein unerfüllter Wunsch. Wratislaw
erhob ebenfalls den Wischehrad, die zweite Burg auf
Prager Gelände, zu einem Repräsentationssitz, der in
vielerlei Hinsicht mit der Prager Burg wetteiferte.

Er errichtete hier die St.-Peter-und-Paul-Kirche
und wenigstens zwei weitere Kirchen. Die Prager
Vorstadt, die der jüdische Händler aus dem spani-
schen Tortosa Ibrahim ibn Jakub um 965 ausführlich
in seiner Reisebeschreibung darstellt, entwickelt sich
in der ausgedehnten Agglomeration beider Burgen.

Im 12. Jahrhundert nahm Prag schrittweise die
Züge einer romanischen Stadt an. Wenn es auch kein
Stadtgebilde im Sinne des Wortes war, besaß es
durch seine Ausdehnung, schöne Bauart und
wirtschaftliche Bedeutung Zentralfunktion von
europäischer Wichtigkeit. In dieser Zeit wurde
die Prager Burg großzügig erneuert, die Judith-
Steinbrücke errichtet, und die Stadt unter der Burg
zählt bereits Dutzende Steinhäuser, die entweder

Unterkünfte der Städter oder Höfe der Adeligen
waren. Das Territorium war bereits verhältnismäßig
dicht mit romanischen Kirchen einzelner Dörfer
und Siedlungen besetzt. Es kam auch zu einer um-
fangreichen Klostergründung. 1142 wurde auf
Initiative des Prager Bischofs das Strahover
Prämonstratenserkloster gegründet. Nach 1158 errichteten die Johanniter am Fuße der Brücke am Kleinseitner Ufer ihre Kommende. Am gegenüberliegen-
den Brückenkopf ließ sich bald auch der heimische
Kreuzherrenorden nieder. In dieser Zeit hatten
sie bereits ihre gefestigte Stellung und das Ungelt
oder Tein, ein befestigtes Zollamt und Kaufherren-
gehöft, Zentrum des Fernhandels beim Altstädter
Marktplatz mit dem Spital und der Marienkirche,
der Vorläuferin der heutigen Teinkirche. Viele
weitere spätere Kirchenbauten haben in ähnlicher
Weise ihre Wurzeln in dieser Zeit, eingeschlossen
das Patrozinium, das bei späteren baulichen
und funktionellen Veränderungen vielfach erhalten
blieb. Der Reichtum romanischer Sakralarchitektur,
soweit er sich in den Gemäuern erhielt, ist heute
zur Mehrheit bis auf wenige Beispiele durch das
Stilgewand späterer Umbauten unsichtbar. Noch we-
niger ist von der malerischen bzw. der Ausgestaltung
mit Statuen erhalten geblieben, von denen Chroniken
berichten. Lediglich illuminierte Handschriften der
Klosterschreiber bleiben die wichtigste Erinnerung
an diese frühe Zeit schöpferischer Anspannungen
des mittelalterlichen Prags. Das dreizehnte Jahrhundert war die Zeit des allseitigen Erblühens des
böhmischen mittelalterlichen Staates. Die wirtschaftliche Entwicklung schritt Hand in Hand mit der Festi-
gung der Autorität und des Prestiges des böhmischen
Königs, dessen Titel seit 1212 durch die internatio-
nale Anerkennung durch die Goldene sizilianische
Bulle Friedrichs II. als für ewig unantastbar und
vererbbar vervollkommnet wurde. Alle Elemente der
Gesellschaft streben in diesem dynamischen Zeitalter
nach Ausgleich mit der umgebenden Welt. Přemysl
Otakar II., der goldene und eiserne König, griff
bereits fast nach der Kaiserkrone, beherrschte ein bis
zum Adriatischen Meer reichendes Reich. Der Adel,
aus fürstlichem Willen untergeordnete Gefolgs-

männer und Verwalter, erhält eine selbständige
Stellung und bildet umfangreiche Besitztümer
heraus. Dicht sind die gegründeten Städte, die Stütze
der herrschaftlichen Macht und die Achse künftiger
wirtschaftlicher Entwicklung. Doch die Kirche blieb
in diesem Prozeß hinter Position und Nützlichkeit
zurück. 1222 erhielt der Prager Bischof ein wichtiges
Privileg durch König Přemysl I., das geistlichen
Personen, Institutionen und Gütern umfangreiche
Immunität zuerkennt. Das Netz kolonialisierender
Klöster, in dieser Zeit vor allem die der Prämon-
stratenser und Ziesterzienser, beteiligt sich an der
territorialen Restrukturalisierung des Landes, in
den Städten lassen sich die Bettelorden nieder. Dennoch kommt es recht langsam zur Annahme und
Verbreitung des neuen gotischen Stils, nach der
Jahrhundertwende nimmt die Stilwandlung an Stärke
zu. Auch in diesem Zeitabschnitt war Prag das Haupt-
eintrittstor neuer Prinzipien. Große Bauunternehmen,
vor allem der Aufbau des ausgedehnten Klosterareals
der Klarissinnen und Minoriten, das in den 30er Jahren durch die hl. Agnes eröffnet wurde, brachten
neue Anregungen direkt in das Stadtmilieu. Den
Bauten der Mendikanten folgten Ausgestaltung und
Neubauten von Laienkirchen und danach auch die
Errichtung von Stadthäusern. Die Altstadt und bald
auch die Kleinseite erhielten die Stadtrechte, und der
Zustrom an Bewohnern bedingt deren schrittweise
Verwandlung in gotische Städte.

Zu Beginn des 14. Jahrhunderts wirkte bereits in
Prag und auf dem Lande eine Vielzahl von Bauhütten
unterschiedlichster Ausrichtung. In der Zwischenzeit
kam es zu einer dramatischen Veränderung. 1306
wurde der letzte Přemyslide Wenzel III. ermordet.
Nach drei Jahren des Streits und der Kämpfe um das
reiche und bedeutungsvolle Königreich wurde der
Gatte seiner Schwester Elisabeth, der luxemburgi-
sche Prinz Johann, Sohn Kaisers Heinrich VIII.,
böhmischer König. Der umgestüm-mutige Ritter,
geschliffene Gesellschafter, scharfsinnige Diplomat
mit dem Mut zu riskanten Operationen und Herr-
scherabenteuern hob das Prestige des böhmischen
Königs, gleichzeitig hinterließ er ein Land, das er in
vielerlei Hinsicht nicht begriff, vor allem im Hinblick

Konflikt aus, dessen Ereignisse und Folgen die
Schicksale Böhmens und der Prager Städte radikal
und nachhaltig beeinflussen sollten.

Der Niederlage der böhmischen Ständeerhebung
von 1618-20 folgten durch Ferdinand II. veranlaßte
Serien von Repressalien, Konfiszierungen und
schließlich die Ausrufung der Erneuerten Landes-
ordnung. Der Ständestaat ging praktisch unter, die
böhmischen Länder waren fest in die habsburgische
mitteleuropäische Monarchie eingekeilt und die
römisch-katholische Konfession die einzige aus-
gerufene Staatsreligion. Kriegszerstörungen,
Wirtschaftsverfall und katastrophale Abnahme der
Bevölkerung führten zur allmählichen Stagnation,
und das Leben des Landes konsolidierte sich noch
lange nach dem Dreißigjährigen Krieg. Die rekatho-
lisierende Propaganda, die sich im architektonischen und künstlerischen Bereich auf expressiv-
visuelle Dringlichkeit stützte, begann sich allerdings
schon vor der Jahrhundertmitte vor allem in der
Tätigkeit der neuen Orden zu zeigen. An deren
Spitze standen die Jesuiten, die in allen drei Prager
Städten vorteilhafte Positionen für die Errichtung
monumentaler Kollegs und Kirchen einnahmen,
es folgten ihnen weitere antireformatorische Orden
und schließlich erneuerten auch die Konvente der
älteren Orden ihre Sitze, die entweder aus der vorhus-
sitischen Zeit überdauert hatten oder die sich erneut
ihrer Objekte bemächtigten. Die Errichtung von
Klosterarealen, vor allem des Klementinums,
bedeuteten für die Stadtpläne ähnlich radikale
Eingriffe wie in der vorangegangenen Zeit die Errichtung von Adelssitzen, vor allem des Palastes Albrecht
von Wallensteins. Nach der Mitte des 17. Jahrhunderts kommt es zur Erneuerung und zum Umbau der
Befestigungen Prags. In dieser Zeit kommen viele
italienische Bauleute hierher, die sich neben for-
tifikatorischen Arbeiten auch der Gestaltung kirchlicher und weltlicher Neubauten zuwandten. Der
neue Stil zeigt sich schrittweise auch im Bereich
Mobiliar bzw. in den anderen Handwerken, er
verallgemeinert sich und wird heimisch, um an der
Wende vom 17. zum 18. Jahrhundert ausdrucksstarke
Züge des heimischen Hochbarocks anzunehmen. Auf

heimischem Boden wächst bereits das Werk von Christoph und Kilian Ignaz Dientzenhofer, J. B. Santini – Aichl, F. M. Kaňka,die in einigen kurzen Jahrzehnten das Antlitz der Stadt gänzlich verändern. Auch wenn die Imigration der Autoren oder der Import von Projekten, Entwürfen und künstlerischen Werken selbst in dieser Zeit nicht unterbrochen wird, wirkt bereits der genius loci und das Stilantlitz des böhmischen und speziell des Prager Barocks anregend auch auf Autoren aus anderen Ländern. Gleichgültig, ob sie hier gelegentlich oder zeitweise arbeiten, ob sie sich hier niederlassen und sich in weiteren Generationen naturalisieren, die Bemühungen um Synthese und mächtige gefühlsbetonte Wirkung des architektonischen Werks wird von Anbeginn ein mächtiger Impuls barocker Malerei und Bildhauerei.

Die Bildhauer M. B. Braun, F. M. Brokoff und Dutzende weitere sind aktive Protagonisten der neuen stilbezogenen Anstrengungen der böhmischen Bildhauerei, denen auf malerischem Gebiet Persönlichkeiten vom Typ Václav Vavřinec Reiner oder Petr Brandl entsprechen. Großartige Persönlichkeiten des Hochbarocks, denen zahlreiche Schüler und oft auch Söhne und Enkel folgten, legten die Grundlagen für die ein Jahrhundert dauernde und über die Zeitengrenzen hinaus wirkende Tradition als aktives Element der böhmischen künstlerischen Erbschaft. Ermüdung und Dämpfung und der Rationalismus Ende des Jahrhunderts und die nachfolgende Epoche der Napoleonischen Kriege zeichnen eine Wende vor.

Prag lebte seit den 20er Jahren des 19. Jahrhunderts bereits ein vom Zeitalter des Barocks unterschiedliches Leben. Der Klassizismus schrieb sich bei sakraler Architektur gewissermaßen nur mit Randnotizen ein. Die vom Interesse an der nationalen Vergangenheit getragene Welle des Romantismus äußert sich vor allem im literarischen und musikalischen Schaffen. Größte Tat dieser Zeit war das Wirken der Gesellschaft für die Beendigung des St.-Veits-Doms. Der Torso der Parlerschen Kirche war schon seit Ende des Mittelalters Gegenstand der Bemühungen um Baubeendigung. Der letzte Versuch um den Abschluß der barocken Bauweiterführung von 1673 blieb in den Anfängen stecken. Erst nunmehr gelang es bis 1873, zu reparieren und danach die dreischiffige Kirche und die westlichen Doppeltürme zu beenden. Die ursprüngliche puristische Auffassung J. Mockers gelang es, mit der Berufung K. Hilberts zu überwinden und ein wirkungsvolles Werk unter Erhalt des ursprünglichen Baubestands in seiner möglichen authentischen Gestalt zu schaffen und ihm funktionell und organisch die Ergebnisse des neuen künstlerischen Schaffens einzufügen. Auch die Wischehrader Kirche machte eine Regotisierung durch. Eine ganze Reihe von Kirchen, vor allem die in den Vorstädten, wurden durch historische Stile inspiriert. Sie entstanden im Laufe des 19. Jahrhunderts außerhalb des historischen Kerns. Die Vorstädte wurden selbständige Städte und wuchsen alsbald in das territoriale und Verwaltungsganze von Groß-Prag.

Im Verlauf des zwanzigsten Jahrhunderts kam es bereits schon nicht mehr zu bemerkenswerten Veränderungen. Die Aufmerksamkeit im Rahmen des Kirchenbaus war vor allem auf deren Instandhaltung und Restaurierung der künstlerischen Ausgestaltung sowie des Mobiliars gerichtet. Nur in den Zeiten zwischen zwei Kriegen entstehen einige selbständige katholische Kirchenobjekte und einzelne evangelische Kirchen. Einige von ihnen gehören zu den bemerkenswerten Realisationen der architektonischen Avantgarde der Zwischenkriegszeit. Prag entkam den Zerstörungen des zweiten Weltkrieges, das einzige beschädigte Kloster, das Emmauskloster, war auch nach Jahren dessen Memento.

SACRAL buildings form one of the fundamental characteristics and a striking elements of historical Prague. The silhouette of the city is interspersed with verticals practically everywhere no matter from where it is viewed. From the four steeples of St. Vitus's Cathedral rising high above the city and a forest of Gothic towers, turrets and belfries to the cupolas and domes of Baroque church buildings they lend rhythm to the relief of the city. The façades of big triple-naved parish and convent churches, living reminders of the medieval appearance of Prague, protrude with strict momentousness into medieval streets, lanes and squares. With emotive urgency the façades of Baroque churches and older buildings masked by the Baroque style catch the eye of passersby. And, finally, Romanesque buildings, scattered and preserved in a small number only, bring to mind the greatness of the town from the times when it began to grow to its later glory and greatness.

This book affords a brief survey of Prague's sacral architecture – for its own value and also because it reflects the complicated masonry of the history of the city as well as the various changes in the life of its inhabitants and big transformations, tensions and breaks of historic significance.

Due to its central position Prague was predetermined to become the seat of the central ruling power and the centre of the spiritual, cultural and economic life of the country. None of this can be imagined from the very beginning without the active participation of the wide clergy, beginning with the bishop and his court and chapters with the institutions of various confraternities up to a number of parish ministers in all the towns of Prague.

<

Prälatur des Kreuzherrenklosters und die St.-Franziskus-Kirche, im Hintergrund die Fassade von St. Salvator.	The prelature of the monastery of the Knights of the Cross and St. Francis's Church. Seen in the background is the façade of the Church of the Holy Saviour.

Reversely, the position of the ruler and the economic prosperity of the city created conditions for continuously developing building enterprise with growing cultural ambitions whose foreground was occupied just by the construction and decoration of holy buildings of diverse missions and purposes.

Not only the sphere of spiritual administration lay in the hands of the clergy. Beginning with the earliest phases of development of the Czech medieval state its members played a role in its management, the running of the sovereign's office and activities in the sphere of diplomacy. From the end of the first millenium the Latin school attached to the St. Vitus Chapter, the highest place of learning until the founding of a university by Charles IV, was active in these fields. It is characteristic that its chancellor was Prague's first archbishop, Arnošt of Pardubice, an exceptionally erudite personality with a broad outlook who was the Emperor and King Charles's chancellor for many years.

The building enterprise of the church, the ruler and finally private founders provided the country with new impulses as regards architectural styles and it was particularly in Prague that the process of the reception, domestication and rooting of new style systems and creative inventions took place. And from Prague the new creative charges spread to the whole of Bohemia and on more than one occasion also to its environs and more remote regions.

The intellectual world of Europe, interwoven with a network of monasteries of various orders, whose number grew continuously and gradually took root in Bohemia, was mediated by individual monks or whole convents arriving in the country, pilgrimages and the journeys of members of the clergy to foreign countries and ultimately regular order chapters. A strong stimulus in this sphere was also the founding of a university, a generally accessible institution of learning which enabled eager minds to absorb – in the course of one generation – the intellectual ferment of the century and to formulate and influence it significantly.

The Hussite movement and the following two centuries of the reformation and renascence of culture created a dividing line between Prague of the Middle Ages and its radical Baroque transformation. After the Peace of Westphalia the recatholization endeavours of the victorious Hapsburgs were soon transferred from the administrative and repressive aspects to active, all-round propaganda which at the end of the century culminated in the explosion of the High Baroque. This changed the appearance of Prague through the building of scores of new places of worship and monasteries and the extensive and often radical reconstruction of medieval buildings. The number of church buildings, considerably large even previously, was considerably over-dimensioned for the conditions of the town in the late 18th century. A period of reduction set in, started by the reforms of the enlightened absolutist Emperor Joseph II. Monasteries in particular were affected by these reforms. In the course of the 19th century, when Prague changed from a lethargic provincial idyll into a bustling centre of industrial enterprise and trade and the revival of the national cultural and political life, its architectural development was sadly marked by the destruction of a number of buildings which although mostly small in size were of irreplaceable historical value. However, at the end of the century the principles of the modern protection of monuments began to prevail and consequently the greater part of Prague's church monuments retained their own cultural and documentary value and, furthermore, their significance in the context of the historical core of the city.

Prague's churches not only represent a stone chronicle and architectural gems, but also an inexhaustible wealth of paintings, sculptures, movables, liturgical vessels, musical and literary monuments, monumental creations and small gems.

Now they are again coming to life as places of church gatherings and personal contemplation, but at the same time they are enjoying the interest of crowds of people coming to admire their formal communication and historical message, or to listen to the tones of old musical compositions.

The development of the early feudal Czech state intermingled with the church history of the country from the very beginning. The process of unification

Blick über die Kleinseitner Dächer
und das Kloster des hl. Thomas
auf die Prager Burg.

View across the Little Quarter
rooftops and St. Thomas's Monastery
towards Prague Castle.

of Bohemia under the supreme rule of the Přemyslid princes went hand in hand with Christianization. This came about shortly after the year 880, when Bořivoj I, a prince of the tribe of Czechs, was christened in Moravia by the bishop St. Methodius. When he took over, with the help of Moravia, firm rule in Bohemia he built the first Christian places of worship – first of all the little Church of St. Clement at his family seat, Levý Hradec, and later the Church of Our Lady in Prague – patently a place of pre-Christian cult and tribal assemblies – which he usurped, founding the Prague castle site, later Prague Castle, here.

Throughout the whole of the dramatic 10th century the Přemyslids continued to build new seats. Bořivoj's son Vratislav founded the oldest Church of St. George – the burial place of the family princes for the following two centuries. Later Václav, the nephew built the oldest church consecrated to the new provincial saint, St. Vitus – a rotunda on the site of St. Wenceslas's Chapel of the present. Prince Václav (Wenceslas) clearly endeavoured to secure greater in-dependence of the church in his country, so far subor-dinated to the Regensburg bishopric, just as he inclined away from subordination to the Duke of Bavaria to cooperation with the Saxon dynasty. At the end of 935 the plotting of magnates brought the aims and the life of Prince Václav to an end. However, before long he and his grandmother Ludmila were made saints.

The importance of Václav the saint, a family and provincial patron, a mystic ruler and intercessor of the Czech lands from whom princes and kings derived their power, exceeded by far, beyond the boundaries of the ages, the prince's short period of earthly reign. Boleslav I, his younger brother and a repentant par-ticipant in the plot to kill him, continued to wage his brother's politics after the consolidation of conditions in the country. His son Boleslav II was successful in getting Prague raised to a bishopric with the consent of the Holy See. The mission to Rome was headed by the prince's sister Mlada, who returned to Prague as a nun and the first abbess of the convent of nuns of the order of St. Benedict attached to St. George's Church. The second convent of the order of St. Benedict was founded in 993 in Břevnov by

Boleslav II on the incentive of Bishop Vojtěch, who before long became a martyr and the third domestic saint. The origin of the bishopric was accompanied by the founding of a metropolitan chapter attached to St. Vitus's Church.

The Přemyslid state continued to grow stronger in the course of the 11th century. After the middle of the century Spytihněv II endeavoured to achieve the independence of the church by founding an archbishopric for the Czech principality as had already been the case in neighbouring Hungary and Poland. For this reason he began the construction of a new church on the site of Václav's rotunda. It was completed in the form of an imposing basilica with two chancels by his brother Vratislav II, the first Czech king. The archdiocese remained an unfulfilled dream until the mid-14th century, however. Vratislav also raised Vyšehrad, the other castle on the territory of Prague, to a representative seat which could compete with Prague Castle in many respects.

He built the chapter Church of SS. Peter and Paul and at least two other churches here. By now Prague's outer bailey, widely mentioned already about the year 965 by the Jewish merchant Ibrahim ibn Jakub of Tortosa in Spain in his book of travels, was developing into a big agglomeration between the two castles.

In the 12th century Prague gradually began to acquire the appearance of a Romanesque town. Even though it was not a municipal formation in the real sense of the word its size, architectural beauty and economic importance made it a centre of European significance. At that time Prague Castle was restored on a large scale, the stone Judith Bridge was built and scores of stone houses sprang up, whether in the form of burghers' dwellings or magnates' courts. Prague's territory was by now relatively densely scattered with small Romanesque churches belonging to the individual villages and communities. Monasteries were also founded on a wide scale. In 1142 a Premonstratensian monastery was founded on the incentive of the bishop of Prague. After 1158 the Johannites built their commendum at the foot of the bridge on the Little Quarter (Malá Strana) side. Finally, the domestic order of the Knights of the Cross settled on the opposite of the bridge. By this time Ungelt, or Týn – the princes' fortified customs-house and merchants' court and a centre of long-distance trade adjoining the Old Town market-place with a hospital and the Church of Our Lady, the predecessor of present-day Týn Church – had its own strong position.

Similarly, many other later church buildings have their roots in this period, including the patrocina, which frequently remained preserved in spite of later architectural and functional changes.

The wealth of Romanesque sacral architecture, if preserved in masonry, is now, apart from a few exceptions, mostly concealed as the result of later reconstructions carried out in various styles. Even less has been preserved of the painted and sculptured decorations, about which chronicles tell us, of the churches concerned. Only illuminated manuscripts from monastery scriptoria continue to be the chief reminder of this early period of the creative upsurge of medieval Prague.

The 13th century was marked by the all-round development of the medieval Czech state. Its economic development was accompanied by con-solidation of the authority and prestige of the Czech king, whose title was indisputable and inheritable for all time as the result of the recognition of Friedrich II in the form of the Golden Bull of Sicily. In that dynamic period all components of the then society en-deavoured to equal the surrounding world. Přemysl Otakar II, the "golden and iron king", now almost reached for the imperial crown and governed an em-pire stretching as far as the Adriatic Sea. The nobility, subordinated on the prince's will to the armed mem-bers of his retinue and administrators, became a separate and independent Estate and formed large dominions. A dense network of towns, the support of the ruler's power and the axis of economic develop-ment in the future, was founded. And the church did not lag behind in this course of things as regards its position and use. In 1222 the bishop of Prague was granted a significant privilege by King Přemysl I ac-cording to which he bestowed extensive immunities on clerical persons, institutions and Estates. The net-work of colonization monasteries, at that time mainly

Blick von den Hradschiner Wällen
auf das Kapuzinerkloster
und das Loreto,
im Hintergrund rechts die Türme
vom Strahov-Kloster.

View of the Capuchin monastery and
the Loretto from the fortification
walls of Hradčany. On the right
in the background are the steeples
on Strahov.

Premonstratensian and Cistercian, participated in the territorial restructuralization of the countryside, followed by mendicant orders in towns. In spite of this the adoption and spreading of the new Gothic style came about relatively slowly, but the change in style gained in strength after the mid-13th century. Prague was the main supporter of new principles also in this period. Large-scale building activities, in particular the construction of the big convent area of the Poor Clares nuns and Minorites, commenced in the thirties by St. Agnes, brought new impulses directly to the town environment. The buildings of the mendicants were followed by modifications of existing or the construction of new lay churches and finally also the erection of town houses. The Old Town and later the Little Quarter gained town rights and the flood of inhabitants conditioned their gradual transformation into Gothic towns.

In the early 14th century a considerable number of building workshops of diverse orientation were already active in Prague. In the meantime a dramatic change had come about. In 1306 the last member of the Přemyslid dynasty, Václav III, was murdered. After three years of disputes and conflicts concerning the wealthy and important kingdom the consort of Václav's sister Eliška, Prince John of Luxembourg, son of the Emperor Heinrich VIII, became Czech king. This bold knight, a refined person and ingenious diplomat who dared to carry out risky operations and had no fear of princely adventures, raised the prestige of the Czech king, but at the same time he left the country, which he did not understand in many respects, at the will of those who by means of high credits and remunerations were able to saturate his military and sovereign undertakings. A turn came about in 1333 when he entrusted his seventeen-years-old son Charles, the later Czech king and Roman Emperor Charles IV, to represent him in the rule of the country. This erudite and, for his age, ambitious Czech prince raised the central power, which had declined, consolidated the country from the economic aspect and contributed to a great extent to the revival of spiritual life while still acting as his father's co-ruler up to 1346.

In 1344 he succeeded in getting Pope Clement VI to raise Prague to an archdiocese and at the same time he moved King John to use one tenth of the gains from the Kutná Hora silver mines for the building of a new cathedral. When this work was taken up by the young Peter Parler in 1352 Charles proved his exceptional ability to select a personality corresponding to the size of the set task. Peter Parler became not only the magister fabricae of St. Vitus's Cathedral and the designer of new, bold plans, but also the leading personality in the realization of other projects of Charles IV who, together with a large retinue of artists, both home and foreign, changed the character of Prague and the country as a whole and contributed to the exceptionally fruitful and widespread culmination of the Czech Gothic. Charles's founding activity reached its climax with the grandiosely conceived enlargement of Prague. Through the founding of the New Town (Nové Město) and the growth of the territory of the Little Quarter Prague's area made the city the third in Europe – after Constantinople and Rome. Building activity also proceeded in the area of the built-up Old Town (Staré Město) and the Little Quarter. However, in the New Town, whose appearance and structure were determined by an unknown urban planner with unusual ingenuity, we can perceive the sovereign's ambitions and conception as its founder.

The period of reign of Charles IV was marked by a dramatic shift in the European intellectual world. New streams of philosophical thinking and endeavours to modify the church and secular order penetrated into Bohemia continuously more intensively, doing so through the mediation of the imperial court and the university founded by Charles IV in 1348. The attention of believers was drawn to an ever greater extent to the words of the preachers avowing the new ideas. Their number included, for example, Konrad Waldhauser and Jan Milíč of Kroměříž, who were followed by a number of masters of Prague University and other priests up to the decisive and uncompromising sermons of Master Jan Hus (John Huss), in whose activity the learned heresy of university teachers combined with popular heresy to form a compact intellectual system. After Hus's death by burning events rapidly surged ahead until the revolutionary explosion in 1419.

The period of the Hussite wars naturally meant the stagnation of artistic activity. The battles waged in Prague marked all three towns and the two castles with numerous destructions and the destroying of movables and rich decorations. There was no thought of the continuation of building and artistic activity even after the Hussite wars and this state of affairs prevailed for a long time. The intellectual world of contemporaries was wholly engaged with problems of dogmatics and the country, devastated by wars and internal conflicts, only gradually recovered to new prosperity after the mid-15th century. Partly built buildings were completed and damaged ones were repaired and in time painting, sculpture and, at the time of Charles IV and Václav IV, flourishing artistic crafts came to the fore, marking the late arrival of the Gothic epoch. As regards the number of the population, there was a surplus of church buildings for the needs of the Utraquist church and the Catholic minority especially in Prague. Thus the Late Gothic movement, headed by outstanding personalities such as Hans Spiess, Benedikt Ried or Matěj Rejsek, mostly found application in secular architecture, or in the completion and repair of old church buildings.

The Renaissance period, whose influence reached Bohemia logically belatedly from the early 16th century, also did not manifest itself to a greater extent in Prague's sacral architecture even though, especially from the end of the seventies, when Prague became the seat of Rudolph II's imperial court, the city was transformed into one of the European centres of manneristic culture and the growing self-assurance of the Catholic minority asserted itself in the interior decoration of numerous older buildings. The greatest building activity of this period was the restoration of the former Dominican monastery by Charles Bridge where in 1556, on the basis of a permit granted by Ferdinand I, the Jesuits settled. In the years 1578 to 1601 they built the triple-naved Church of the Holy Saviour. In the Rudolphian period large-scale immigration, particularly from Italy, the Netherlands and German countries, gave rise to the origin of

several buildings. At the end of the century the Italians who had settled in Prague founded the Italian Congregation, which established a hospital with the Church of St. Charles Borromaeus and, in the immediate vicinity of the Clementinum, the oval Chapel of the Assumption of Our Lady. The German Lutherans also built two churches – one consecrated to the Holy Trinity in the Little Quarter (now the Church of Our Lady Victorious) and the other to the Holy Saviour in the Old Town. By now, however, the European conflict represented by the Thirty Years' War was approaching whose course and results were of a radical character and marked the destiny of Bohemia and the town of Prague for all time. The defeat of the uprising of the Czech Estates of 1618 to 1620 was crowned by Ferdinand II's series of repressions, confiscations and, finally, the declaration of the renewed provincial administration. The state of the Estates virtually ceased to exist, the Czech lands were firmly wedged in the Central European monarchy of the Hapsburgs and the Roman Catholic faith was declared to be the only state religion. The war destruction, the disruption of the economy and the catastrophic decrease in the number of the population led to a long drawn-out period of stagnation and the life of the country was in a constant process of consolidation long after the termination of the Thirty Years' War.

However, re-Catholization propaganda based on expressive visual urgency in the spheres of architecture and art began to manifest itself in the activity of anti-Reformation orders. These were headed by the Jesuits, who in all three towns of Prague occupied advantageous positions for the building of monumental

<

Kleinseitner Ring. Der intime Raum und der kleine Maßstab der Stadthäuser kontrastieren mit der barocken Dominante. | Malostranské Square. The intimacy of the square and the small scale of the burghers' houses form a contrast with the Baroque landmark.

colleges and churches. They were followed by other anti-reformation orders and ultimately older orders which had either survived from the pre-Hussite period, or had newly taken over their buildings and renewed their seats and convents. The construction of monastery areas, in particular the Clementinum, affected the ground-plan structure of the town just as radically as the building of residences of the nobility, especially the palace of Albrecht of Wallenstein, had done in the preceding period. After the mid-17th century the fortifications of Prague were renewed and reconstructed. In this period numerous Italian builders arrived in the country who, apart from work on the fortifications, devoted their attention to the modification and construction of sacral and secular buildings. The new style was gradually projected into the sphere of movables and other crafts, becoming generally rooted and domesticated in order to acquire the characteristic features of the Czech High Baroque at the turn of the 17th and 18th centuries. The work of Kryštof and Kilián Ignác Dientzenhofer, J. B. Santini Aichl and F. M. Kaňka, who changed the appearance of the town in just a few decades, grew from home soil. Although the immigration of architects and artists and the import of plans, designs and works of art did not come to an end even in this period, the genius loci now asserted itself and the character of the Czech and especially the Prague Baroque had an incentive influence on architects and artists of other countries regardless of whether they worked here incidentally or occasionally, or settled here and became naturalized in later generations. From the very beginning an endeavour to achieve a synthesis and a powerful emotional effect of an architectural work was the strong impulse of Baroque painting and sculpture. The sculptors M. B. Braun, F. M. Brokoff and scores of others were active protagonists of the new aims of Czech sculpture as regards style, their counterparts in the sphere of painting being personalities of the type of Václav Vavřinec Reiner or Petr Brandl. The great personalities of the High Baroque were followed by numerous pupils and very often their sons and nephews laid the foundation of a tradition which survived for a whole century and exerted an influence beyond the boundaries of the ages as an active component of the Czech art tradition.

The fatigue and rationalism of the end of the century and finally the epoch of the Napoleonic Wars meant a dividing line.

From the nineties of the 19th century Prague lived a life which differed from the Baroque era. Classicism inscribed itself in sacral architecture only marginally. The wave of Romantism, borne by interest in the national past, chiefly manifested itself in literary and musical works. The greatest activity in this period was realized by the Union for the Completion of St. Vitus's Cathedral. Since the late Middle Ages endeavours had been made to complete the torso of Peter Parler's cathedral, the last attempt to finish the work in the Baroque style in 1673 coming to a halt at its very beginning. Only now were the triple-naved building and the two western steeples completed to mark the millennium of St. Wenceslas. With the summoning of Kamil Hilbert the puristic conception of Josef Mocker was overcome, an effective work originating which preserved the original parts of the building in their authentic form to the greatest possible extent. This work was enhanced purposefully and organically by the results of new building activities. The church on Vyšehrad underwent a process of re-Gothicization. A number of suburban churches which had originated on the periphery of the historical core in the 19th century were inspired by historical styles. Separate towns were built which finally spread into the territorial and administrative whole of Greater Prague.

No striking changes have come about in the course of the 20th century. As regards church buildings, attention is mostly concentrated on their maintenance and the restoration of their artistic decorations and movables. The period between the two World Wars alone was marked by the origin of several independent Catholic church buildings and buildings of individual Evangelic churches. Some of them rank among the remarkable realizations of avant-garde architects of the said period. Prague virtually escaped the destruction of the Second World War, only the damaged "Na Slovanech" monastery being its memento for a number of years.

Das Barockinterieur lebt vom eigenwilligen Zusammenspiel von Licht, Farben und unterschiedlichen Materialien. Statuen von M. B. Braun in der St.-Klemens-Kirche.

>

Silhouette der Altstadt – Dutzende Vertikale bestimmen ihren Charakter. Blick vom Brückenturm nach Osten.

This Baroque interior creates an effective impression in a rare play of light, colours and different materials.

>

The outline of the Old Town is characterized by scores of high spires. View from the bridge tower towards the east.

ALTSTADT | THE OLD TOWN

An der Verbindungslinie zwischen den beiden Fürstenburgen Prag und Vyšehrad entwickelte sich seit dem 11. Jahrhundert der Kern des künftigen Prags. Hierher verlagerte sich der Hauptmarktplatz von der Vorburg, hier entstanden auch Ansiedlungen fremder Kaufherren. Als die Altstadt in den 30er Jahren des 13. Jahrhunderts die Stadtrechte zugesprochen bekam und mit Maner umgeben wurde, war sie bereits von Dutzenden Kirchen und Klosterarealen besetzt. Bis Mitte des 14. Jahrhunderts war ihre urbanistische Entwicklung im Grunde abgeschlossen. Nur wenige neue Kirchen und Klöster kamen hinzu, dafür wurden ältere Objekte erneuert und erweitert. Überstieg doch deren Anzahl die Bedürfnisse der Stadt bedeutend ebenso wie ihre kulturelle Bedeutung und der Einfluß des Geschehens in ihren Mauern.

From the 11th century the core of Prague of the future developed on the communication between the two princes' castles – Prague and Vyšehrad. The central market-place was transferred here from the outer bailey and communities of foreign merchants sprang up here. When the Old Town was granted town rights and surrounded by fortification walls in the thirties of the 13th century it was already scattered with scores of churches and monastery areas. Up to the mid-14th century its urban development was in essence completed. Only a negligible number of new church and monastery buildings originated, but on the other hand older buildings were restored and enlarged throughout whole centuries. Indeed, their number considerably exceeded the needs of the town similarly as the cultural significance and influence of the events taking place within their walls.

Die Ostfront des Altstädter Rings wird durch die zweischiffige Marienkirche vor dem Tein bestimmt. Vor deren Fassade befindet sich das Gebäude der ehemaligen Tein-Pfarrschule aus dem 14.-16. Jh. Links von ihr das Haus zur Steinernen Glocke, ein erst vor kurzem rekonstruierter frühgotischer Bau, ein Mitte des 14. Jh. prächtig umgebautes Stadthaus.

>
Marienkirche vor dem Tein, Blick durch das Hauptschiff zum Abschluß. Das ursprüngliche Gewölbe wurde nach dem Brand von 1679 durch ein barockes ersetzt. Das einzigartige Interieur der Teinkirche verbindet in seiner überwältigenden funktionellen und gestalterischen Geschlossenheit Elemente der Gotik, Renaissance und des Barocks.

The eastern front of Old Town Square is dominated by the twin-towered Church of Our Lady of Týn. In front of its façade stands the building of the former Týn parish school of the 14th-16th centuries, On its left is the house called At the Stone Bell (U kamenného zvonu), recently reconstructed in Early Gothic style. In the mid-14th century it was a luxurious burgher's house.

>
The Church of Our Lady of Týn, view from the main nave towards the east. The original vault was replaced with a Baroque one after a fire in 1679. The unique interior of Týn Church combines the functional and decorative elements of the Gothic, Renaissance and Baroque to form a captivating whole.

TEINKIRCHE
Der Altstädter Ring war seit altersher ein zentraler Raum, um den die Altstadt emporwuchs. Er war Marktplatz von europäischer Bedeutung, Versammlungsstätte, Schauplatz berühmter und grausamer Ereignisse von geschichtlicher Bedeutung, die sich im Schatten des Altstädter Rathauses und der Teinkirche abspielten.

THE CHURCH OF OUR LADY OF TÝN
From ancient times Old Town Square was the central space around which the Old Town grew. It was a market-place of European significance, an important meeting-place and the scene of illustrious and cruel events taking place at the foot of the Old Town Hall and Týn Church.

TEINKIRCHE

Durchblick vom Hochgewölbe zum Priesterraum
und die Gegenperspektive des Fensterabschlusses
zeugt von der spannungsvollen Eigenart der
Hochgotik in Böhmen etwa Mitte des 14. Jahrhunderts
und vom Selbstbewußtsein der Altstädter Bewohner.
Sie erhielten erst 1338 die Rechte zur Einrichtung
eines Rathauses und schritten bereits kurz danach zur
Errichtung einer neuen Hauptkirche, die die alte
dreischiffige aus dem 13. Jahrhundert ersetzte.
Vorgänger beider Kirchen war geringere
romanische Kirche.

THE CHURCH OF OUR LADY OF TÝN

The view through the top of the vault into the presbytery
and the oppositely oriented perspective
of the windows of the east end bear witness to
the spiritual upsurge of the culminating Gothic in
Bohemia about the mid-14th century and the self-confidence
of the Old Town burghers. Not until 1338 did they gain
the right to found a Town Hall, shortly afterwards
commencing the construction of a new main church which
replaced the older triple-naved building
of the 13th century. The predecessor of both was
a small Romanesque church.

Altstadt | The Old Town

TEINKIRCHE

Sie grenzte an das Spital der ausländischen Kaufherren beim fürstlichen Zollamt an – dem Tein oder Ungelt. Seit 1427, als hier der Hussitenprediger Jan Rokycana wirkte, der spätere kalixtinische Erzbischof, war die Kirche Mittelpunkt des böhmischen Utraquismus. In ihren Giebel wurde ein vergoldeter Kelch und die Plastik des Königs Georg von Poděbrad eingefügt, die 1626 durch die Statue der Madonna im Heiligenschein ersetzt wurde. An der Errichtung und Ausgestaltung der Kirche waren im 14. Jh. die Hütte Peter Parlers und die Baumeister Wenzels IV. beteiligt.

THE CHURCH OF OUR LADY OF TÝN

This church belonged to the hospital of foreign merchants attached to the princes' customs-house – called Týn or Ungelt. From 1427, when the Hussite priest Jan Rokycana, later to become the Utraquist archbishop, preached here, the church was the centre of Czech Utraquism. Situated on its gable was a gilded chalice and a statue of King George of Poděbrady, replaced in 1626 with a sculpture of the Madonna with a halo. Peter Parler's workshop and court masters of Václav IV participated in the building and decoration of the church in the 14th century.

TEINKIRCHE
Die Innengestaltung der Teinkirche erhält ihre besonderen Züge vor allem durch eine Kollektion frühbarocker Altäre. Der Hauptaltar mit Gemälden von Karel Škréta von 1649 stellt ein Spitzenbeispiel des Frühbarocks in Prag dar. Von den ursprünglichen Steinstatuen sind besonders bemerkenswerte Sedile vom Beginn des 15. Jh. in den Abschlußseitenschiffen und das Nordportal der Kirche, ein Werk der Hütte Peter Parlers um 1390 (das Original befindet sich in der Nationalgalerie.)

THE CHURCH OF OUR LADY OF TÝN
The character of the interior of Týn Church is given by a remarkable group of Early Baroque altars. The high altar with paintings by Karel Škréta of 1649 is a peak sample of the Early Baroque in Prague. Remarkable among the stone sculptures are the sedilia of the early 15th century in the east end of the side naves and the nothern portal of the church, the work of Peter Parler's workshop of about 1390 (the original is deposited in the National Gallery).

Altar des Nordschiffes mit Statuen der gotischen Kalvarie, ein Werk des Meisters der Kreuzigung vom Tein vom Beginn des 15. Jahrhunderts. Zusammen mit der Kanzel und dem Taufbecken aus Zinn im Südschiff aus dem Jahre 1414 gehört sie zum ältesten erhaltenen Teil der ursprünglich gotischen Ausgestaltung und des ehemaligen Inventars.

The altar in the northern aisle with sculptures portraying a Gothic Calvary, the work of the Master of the Týn Crucifixion of the early 15th century. Along with the pulpit and the tin font in the southern aisle of 1414 it is the oldest preserved part of the original Gothic decorations and furnishings.

Die Teinkirche war auch wichtige Begräbnisstätte. Hier ruht der Erzbischof Jan Rokycana, in der Mitte der Kirche steht ein spätgotischer Baldachin des Weihbischofs Mirandola, hier haben auch der weise Astronom Tycho de Brahe und der jüdische Konvertit Simon Abeles ihre Grabmale.

Týn Church was an important burial place. The archbishop Jan Rokycana was laid to rest here and standing in the centre of the church is the Late Gothic baldachin of Bishop Mirandola. The renowned astronomer Tycho Brahe and the Jewish convert Šimon Abeles are brought to mind by their tombstones here.

ST. JAKOB DER GRÖSSERE
Der Blick von Osten auf die Konventkirche
der Minoriten. St. Jakob der Größere verrät bis heute,
daß sie in ihrer Entstehungszeit (1374 geweiht)
eines der Spitzenwerke der luxemburgischen Gotik
und eine der größten Prager Kirchen war.
Die hochbarocke Gestaltung der Kirche gelang es,
mit der räumlichen Konzeption der mendikantischen
Architektur und deren wirkungsvoller Kraft in
der Raumauffassung und des Mobiliars auszugleichen.
Weitberühmte Orgel aus dem Jahre 1705.

THE CHURCH OF ST. JAMES THE GREATER
The view from the east of the convent Church
of St. James the Great of the Minorites still betrays
the fact that at the time of its origin (consecrated
in 1374) it was one of the peak works of the Luxembourg
Gothic and Prague's biggest church. The High
Baroque modification of the church successfully came to
terms with the spatial conception of
mendicant architecture and its effective power in
the conception of the interior of the building and its
furnishings, including the 1705 organ.

ST. JAKOB DER GRÖSSERE

Die Barockisierung nach dem Brand von 1689
durchlief eine Reihe von Etappen. In der frühen
Phase entstand die Hauptfront mit einer hohen
Pilasterreihe und reicher Stuckverzierung über
dem Portal von O. Mosto 1695.
Die Innengestaltungen wurden bis 1739 ausgeführt.
Gleichzeitig wurde die Disposition der Basilika
durch den Einbau von Emporen in die Seitenschiffe
verändert, dennoch blieb der Eindruck der
Vertikalität und des fliehenden Moments entlang
der Achse erhalten.

THE CHURCH OF ST. JAMES THE GREATER

The Barocization
of the church after a fire which
occurred in 1689 was carried
out in several phases.
In the early phase the main façade
with a pilaster and rich stucco
decoration on the cap of the portal,
the work of O. Mosto of 1695,
originated.

Grabmal des Grafen Johannes Wenzel Wratislaw von Mitrovice, höchster Kanzler des böhmischen Königreichs, eines der bedeutsamsten Denkmäler der funeralen Architektur des barocken Prags von 1714–16, ein Projekt J. B. Fischers von Erlach, plastische Gestaltung F. M. Brokoff.
<

Nördlicher Flügel des Ambits des Minoritenklosters bei St. Jakob 30er Jahre des 14. Jahrhunderts aus der Zeit des Klosterumbaus zu Zeiten Johanns von Luxemburg. Vom ältesten Konventgebäude aus der Gründungszeit des Klosters erhielten sich zwei Gewölbe in den unterirdischen Räumen.

The tombstone of Count Jan Václav Vratislav of Mitrovice, the supreme chancellor of the Czech kingdom. It is one of the most outstanding monuments of funeral achitecture of Baroque Prague – (1714–1716). It was designed by J. B. Fischer von Erlach and its sculptural decoration is the work of F. M. Brokoff.
<

The northern branch of the cloister of the Minorite monastery attached to St. James's Church dates from the 1330's, the time of the reconstruction of the monastery carried out during the reign of John of Luxembourg. Two vaulted rooms in the cellerage of the oldest monastery building dating from the time of the founding of the monastery have been preserved.

ST. JAKOB DER GRÖSSERE
St.-Jakobs-Kloster, gegründet 1232 im Zusammenhang mit der Zuerkennung der Stadtrechte der Altstadt. Es besaß eine außerordentlich große Bedeutung im Leben der mittelalterlichen Stadt. Heute ist es eine der besuchtesten Prager Denkwürdigkeiten - seines einzigartigen Interieurs und der regelmäßig stattfindenden Konzerte wegen nimmt es einen wichtigen Platz im Musikleben der Stadt ein.

THE CHURCH OF ST. JAMES THE GREATER
St. James's Monastery founded in 1232 in connection with the granting of town rights to the Old Town, was an important component of medieval town life. Nowadays it is one of the most frequently visited Prague monuments due to its unique interior. The concerts held here regularly have gained it a permanent place in Prague's musical life.

Die nordwestliche Ecke des Altstädter Rings wird durch die St.-Nikolaus-Kirche beherrscht. Deren Stirnseite mündete allerdings ursprünglich in eine enge Gasse.

The north-western corner of Old Town Square is dominated by St. Nicholas's Church. However, its façade originally faced a narrow lane.

<

ST. NIKOLAUS
Die ursprünglich dreischiffige Basilika wurde durch deutsche Kaufleute zu Beginn des 13. Jh. gegründet, als sie ihre ursprüngliche Siedlung Na poříčí verließen und sich nahe dem zentralen Marktplatz ansiedelten. Nach der Erteilung der Stadtrechte bildete die Pfarrkirche auch Versammlungsstätte, noch vor der Errichtung des Rathauses.

ST. NICHOLAS'S CHURCH
The original triple-naved basilica was founded by German merchants in the early 13th century, when they left their original community (Na Poříčí) and settled near the central market-place. After the granting of town rights the parish church also served as a meeting-place of the burghers before the founding of the Town Hall.

Ihr heutiges Aussehen verlieh der Kirche K. I. Dientzenhofer in den Jahren 1732-35. Die Kuppelfresken schuf der bayerische Maler C. D. Asam, die Figurenausschmückung stammt von Anton Braun, Neffe von Matthias Bernard Braun. Ab 1871 wurde sie durch die russisch-orthodoxe Kirche genutzt. 1920 wurde hier die tschechoslowakische hussitische Kirche ausgerufen, deren Sitz sie wurde.

Its present form is the work of K. I. Dientzenhofer of 1732 to 1735. The frescoes in the cupola are the work of the Bavarian painter K. D. Asam and the sculptural decoration that of Antonín Braun, nephew of Matthias Braun. From 1871 it was used by the Russian Orthodox church. In 1920 the Czechoslovak Hussite church was declared here and the church is its seat.

Links – Westflügel des Ambits
des Klarissen-Klosters. Rechts – Blick zum Abschluß
der Klosterkirche – im Hintergrund die Kirche
des Franziskanerklosters der Minoriten,
im Vordergrund das St.-Salvator-Kloster
der Klarissinnen.

On the left – the western wing of the cloister of the
Convent of the Poor Clares, on the right – view of the
east end of the convent church, in the background
the Minorite Church of St. Francis
and in the foreground the Church of the Holy Saviour
of the Convent of the Poor Clares.

<

AGNESKLOSTER
König Wenzel I. gründete in den Jahren 1233–34
auf ausgedehnten Grundstücken nahe des Moldauufers
auf Veranlassung seiner Schwester der erst vor kurzem
heilig gesprochenen St.-Agnes, Kloster der Klarissinnen
und kurz danach das anliegende Minoritenkloster.
An der Spitze des Konvents stand vorstellungsgemäß
fast ein halbes Jahrhundert lang seine Gründerin.
Es war nicht nur ein Brennpunkt des geistigen Lebens,
inspiriert durch das Lehren des hl. Franziskus von Assisi,
sondern auch der Platz, von wo aus die Gotik als Stil
nach Prag und ganz Böhmen Eingang fand.

THE AGNES CONVENT
In the years 1233 to 1234 King Václav I founded,
on the incentive of his sister Agnes, the recently
canonized, a convent for the Poor Clares on a large
site by the bank of the River Vltava. This was followed
shortly afterwards by the founding of the adjoining
Minorite monastery. For nearly fifty years the Convent
of the Poor Clares was headed by its founder, Agnes,
as its Mother Superior. It was not only a focus of
spiritual life inspired by the teaching of St. Francis
of Assisi, but also the starting point for the advent
of the Gothic style in Prague and Bohemia as a whole.

AGNESKLOSTER

1420 flohen die Klarissinnen aus der durch die Hussiten beherrschten Stadt nach Panenský Týnec, von wo sie 1627 zurückkehrten. 1782 wurde das Kloster durch Josef II. aufgehoben. Das ursprünglich mit eigener Gerichtsbarkeit ausgestattete, nun aus der städtischen Rechtsbefugnis ausgegliederte ausgedehnte Gelände verwandelte sich an der zerfallenden Peripherie allmählich in Lagerstätten, Werkstätten und Behausungen für die ärmsten Prager. Der Verein für die Klostererneuerung bemühte sich seit 1892 darum, dem unaufhaltsamen Verfall des Geländes entgegenzutreten und leistete im Verlauf eines halben Jahrhunderts eine verdienstvolle Arbeit.

THE AGNES CONVENT

In 1420 the Poor Clares fled from the town, now under the rule of the Hussites, to Panenský Týn, from where they returned in 1627. In 1782 Joseph II abolished the convent. The large area, which originally had its own jurisdiction and did not come under municipal authority, became a decaying periphery used for storage purposes, workshops and dwellings for Prague's most destitute inhabitants. From 1892 the Society for the Restoration of the Convent tried to overcome the unarrestable devastation of the Agnes area and carried out meritorious work in the course of half a century.

Altstadt | The Old Town

Links – Rekonstruierter Paradieshof
des Klarissinnenklosters.
Rechts – Blick in das Areal des Agnesklosters von
Westen. Im Vordergrund die Stirnseite des Konvents und
des Spitals des anliegenden Geländes des Ordens der
Barmherzigen Brüder aus der Mitte des 18. Jahrhunderts.

On the left – the reconstructed Court of Paradise
of the Convent of the Poor Clares.
On the right – view of the Agnes area from the west.
In the foreground the façade of the convent and the
hospital of the adjoining area of the order of the
Brothers of Mercy.

<

AGNESKLOSTER
Nach dem zweiten Weltkrieg kam es
zu einer komplexen archäologischen
und bauhistorischen Untersuchung
des Geländes, das seit den 60er
Jahren rekonstruiert und für
die Bedürfnisse der Nationalgalerie
neu gestaltet wurde, die hier einen
Teil ihrer Sammlungen unterbrachte –
die Exposition der tschechischen
Kunst des 19. Jahrhunderts.

THE AGNES CONVENT
After the Second World War the Agnes
area was subjected to complex
archeological and architectural-
historical research. From the sixties
it was reconstructed and modified
for the needs of the National Gallery.
A part of the collections of this
institution – the exposition of 19th
century Czech art –
is now housed in it.

ST. FRANZISKUS

Der Burgunder Jean Baptiste Matthey gab dem barocken Aussehen Prags durch eine Reihe bedeutender Bauten unverwechselbare Züge. Einer der bedeutendsten ist die Kirche St. Franziskus Seraphicus aus den Jahren 1679-89, ein Zentralbau, dessen Kuppel und Fassade zu den charakteristischen Elementen der Stadt gehören. Mattheys Bau ersetzte die ältere Konventkirche des heimischen Ordens, der Spitalbrüder der Kreuzherren mit dem Rotem Stern, entstanden beim Agneskloster und von 1252 an der Brücke angesiedelt.

ST. FRANCIS'S CHURCH

Jean Baptiste Matthey of Burgundy helped to create the Baroque appearance of Prague with a number of outstanding buildings. One of the foremost of them is the Church of St. Francis Seraphicus from 1679 to 1689. It is a central building whose cupola and façade rank among the characteristic elements of the city. Matthey's building replaced an older convent church of a home order, the hospital brotherhood of the Knights of the Cross with a Red Star which originated in connection with the Convent of St. Agnes and which from 1252 had its seat by the bridge.

Fresken des Jüngsten Gerichts in der Kuppel der Kreuzherrenkirche, ein Werk von Václav Vavřinec Reiner (1722–23), ebenso wie die Bilder der Evangelisten und der Kirchenväter zwischen den Bogen der Kirchenschiffe.

The fresco portraying The Last Judgement in the cupola of the church of the Knights of the Cross with a Red Star is the work of Václav Vavřinec Reiner (1722–1723) similarly as the paintings of Evangelists and church fathers between the arches of the nave.

Den Hauptaltar schufen der Bildhauer V. V. Jäckel und der Schreiner J. Dobner 1701, das Gemälde der Brandmarkung des hl. Franziskus J. K. Liška. Die Plastiken in den Pfeilernischen des Schiffes sind ein Werk der Brüder Süssner aus Dresden und M. V. Jäckels.

The high altar is the work of sculptor M. V. Jäckel and woodcarver J. Dobner from 1701 and the painting The Stigmatization of St. Francis that of J. K. Liška. The sculptures in niches in the pillars of the nave are the work of the brothers Süssner of Dresden and M. V. Jäckel.

KLEMENTINUM

1556 kamen Jesuiten nach Prag und besiedelten das bislang dominikanische Kloster an der Karlsbrücke. Die vertriebenen Dominikaner wichen ins Agneskloster und danach auch in den St. Ägidius aus. 1578 begannen die Jesuiten den Bau der St.-Salvator-Kirche, und während mehr als zweier Jahrhunderte erweiterten sie ihr Kolleg, das Klementinum, auf Kosten ganzer Blocks von Stadthäusern bis zu seiner heutigen kolossalen Gestalt.

THE CLEMENTINUM

In 1556 the Jesuits arrived in Prague and occupied the till then Dominican monastery by Charles Bridge. The Dominicans moved to the Agnes Monastery and later to St. Giles's. In 1578 the Jesuits commenced the construction of the Church of the Holy Saviour and in the course of over two centuries enlarged their college – the Clementinum – at the cost of whole blocks of burghers' houses, the result being the colossal building we know today.

Blick durch die
Karlsgasse auf die
Welsche Kapelle
aus den Jahren
1590–97, eingekeilt
zwischen der
St.-Salvator-und
der
St.-Klemens-Kirche.

>
Der Dynamismus
hochbarocker
Formen der zweiten
Kirche im
Klementinum, der
St.-Klemens-Kirche
(projektiert durch
F. M. Kaňka,
1711–15) mit ihrem
selten
ausgewogenen
Interieur des Prager
Barocks,
kontrastiert mit der
Formenwucht der
St.-Salvator-Kirche.

View through
Karlova Street of the
Italian Chapel
(1590–1597),
wedged in a corner
between the Church
of the Holy Saviour
and St. Clement's
Church.

>
The dynamism of
the High Baroque
forms of the other
church in the
Clementinum – St.
Clement's (designed
by F. M. Kaňka,
1711–1715) – forms
a contrast with the
ingenuity of the
forms of the Early
Baroque Church of
the Holy Saviour.

Blick durch die Řásnovka-Gasse, einen malerischen Teil des ehemaligen Castullus-Viertels südlich des Agnes-Klosters zur St.-Castullus-Kirche.
<

View across Řásnovka, a picturesque part of the former Haštal (Castullus) quarter lying south of the Agnes Convent, of the Church of St. Castullus.
<

Hl.-Geist-Kirche, ursprünglich ein Benediktinerkloster, gegründet 1346, zerstört 1420, in der zweiten Hälfte des 16. Jahrhunderts in eine Pfarre verwandelt. Der interessante einschiffige Raum aus der Zeit nach 1350 wurde Ende des 17. Jh. teilweise barock umgestaltet.

The Church of the Holy Spirit, originally a part of the Benedictine convent founded in 1346, abolished in 1420 and in the latter half of the 16th century changed into a parish church. Its interesting single-naved interior dates from after 1350 and was partly modified in the Baroque in the late 17th century.

St.-Castullus-Kirche sie entstand in den 40er bis 70er Jahren des 14. Jahrhunderts. Der ursprünglich dreischiffig begonnene Bau findet seinen Höhepunkt im ausgezeichneten zweischiffigen Interieur im Nordschiff, das zu den Spitzenleistungen der luxemburgischen Gotik in der Prager Architektur gehört.

St. Castullus's Church originated in the forties to the seventies of the 14th century. The building, originally started as a triple-naved one, ended up with an outstanding double-naved interior ranking among the peak manifestations of the Luxembourg Gothic in Prague architecture.

ST. ÄGIDIUS
Die St.-Ägidius-Kirche wurde 1339–71
für das durch Erzbischof Johannes IV.
von Dražice gegründete Kapitel
an der Stelle eines romanischen
Kirchleins des deutschen
Ritterordens gegründet. 1626 ließen
sich hier die Dominikaner nieder,
die die Kirche in den 30er Jahren
barock umgestalteten.
Der dreischiffige Saalinnenraum
gehört zu den schönsten Prager
Barockinterieuren.

ST. GILES'S CHURCH
St. Giles's Church was built
from 1339 to 1371 for the chapter
founded by Bishop Jan IV of Dražice
on the site of a small Romanesque
church of the order of German Knights.
In 1626 the Dominicans settled here
and modified the building in Baroque
style in the thirties.
The hall-type, triple-naved interior
of the church ranks among the most
beautiful samples
of the Prague Baroque.

Die südliche Stirnseite der Bethlehemskapelle läßt nach der Rekonstruktion den ursprünglichen Zustand zur Zeit von Jan Hus und der Zeit um 1521, als hier Thomas Müntzer predigte, wieder entstehen. Ironie des Schicksals - die Kapelle wurde -inzwischen 1661 umgebaut - durch die Jesuiten gekauft. Nach der Ordensaufhebung 1786 wurde sie auf die Grundfesten zerstört. Deren Reste bestimmten zusammen mit archäologischen Resten das heutige Aussehen der Kapelle.
<

Die Hl.-Kreuz-Rotunde vom Beginn des 12. Jahrhunderts ist nicht nur als Beweis frühester Besiedlung der Altsadt anzusehen, sondern auch dafür, wie sie geschützt war - 1860 wandte sich der künstlerische Verein „Umělecká Beseda" gegen ihren Abriß. Dank seines Einsatzes steht sie bis heute auf einer Eckparzelle anstelle eines Mietshauses.

After its reconstruction the southern façade of Bethlehem Chapel evokes an idea of its original state at John Huss's time, and about 1521, when Thomas Münzer preached in the chapel. Through the irony of fate the building, reconstructed in the meantime, was purchased by the Jesuits in 1661. After the abolition of the order the chapel was demolished in 1786, the few remaining fragments of its masonry along with archeological finds determining its present appearance.
<

The Rotunda of the Holy Rood the Smaller of the early 12th century is a remarkable testimony to the significance of the pre-location settlement of the Old Town. Apart from this, it is noteworthy due to the fact that in 1860 the Umělecká beseda art society prevented it from being demolished. Thanks to this society it is still standing on a corner plot of land instead of an intended block of flats.

BETHLEHEMSKAPELLE

1391 gründeten zwei Stadtbürger, der Kaufherr Kříž und Hanuš aus Mühlheim, die Kapelle für tschechische Predigten. Der strenge, flachdeckige Saal brachte seine Mission zum Ausdruck, die sich nach 1402 erfüllte, als Meister Jan Hus Prediger wurde. Das Denkmal der nationalen Geschichte, der böhmischen und europäischen Reformation wurde 1950-52 aus Fragmenten rekonstruiert.

BETHLEHEM CHAPEL

In 1391 two burghers, shopkeeper Kříž and Hanuš of Mülheim, founded this chapel for the preaching of sermons in the Czech language. The moderate, flat-ceilinged hall-type interior of the building expressed its mission, crowned after 1402 when Master John Huss began to preach here. This monument of national history, of the Czech and European reformation, was reconstructed from fragments in the years 1950 to 1952.

1627 wurde die Kirche den Karmelitern zum Geschenk gemacht, die auf den angrenzenden Grundstücken ein Kloster errichteten und die Kirche im Laufe des ersten Drittels des 18. Jahrhunderts barock umgestalteten. Die westliche Stirnseite wurde mit einer illusiv-dynamischen gewellten Kulisse ausgestattet.

>
Blick in das barock ausgestattete Hauptschiff und zum Abschluß der St.-Gallus-Kirche.

In 1627 the church was bestowed on the Carmelites, who built a monastery on the neighbouring plots of land and modified the church in Baroque style in the first third of the 18th century. The western façade of the building was provided with an illusive, dynamically undulated setting.

>
View of the Baroquely modified main nave and and east end of St. Gallus's Church.

ST. GALLUS
Der Ursprung der St.-Gallus-Kirche reicht bis in die 30er Jahre des 13.Jahrhunderts zurück, als das Altstädter Gebiet durch die Herausbildung einer neuen Ansiedlung bereichert wurde - die Nova civitas circa S. Gallum-, die die regelmäßige lokale Parzellierung unter Nutzung der älteren urbanistischen Einteilung nutzte. Die Bedeutung der Kirche wird durch den Umbau zu Zeiten Karls IV. unterstrichen.

ST. GALLUS'S CHURCH
The origin of St. Gallus's Church dates back to the thirties of the 13th century, when the settlement of the territory of the Old Town was completed by the formation of a new community, Nova civitas circa S. Gallum - combining the regular parcelling-out of the location with the use of the older urban layout. The importance of the church was underlined by its reconstruction at the time of Charles IV.

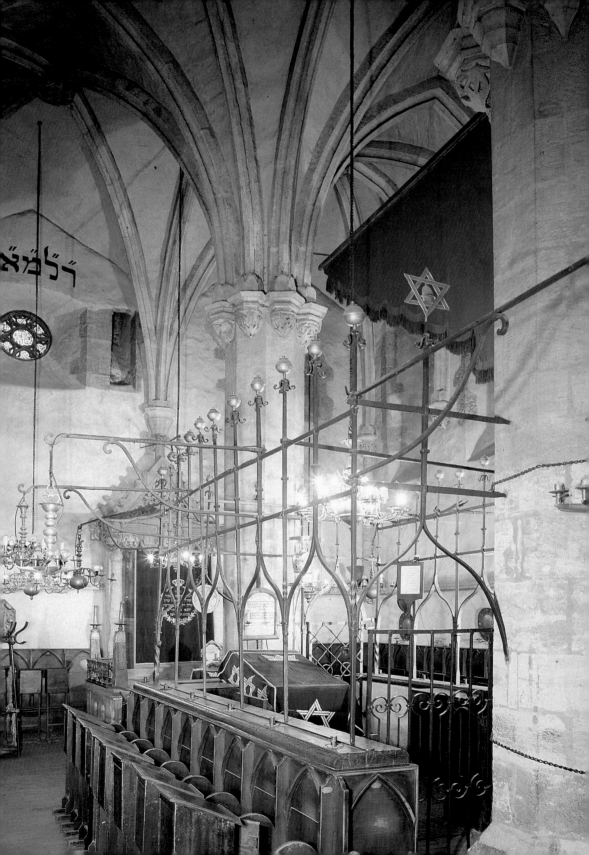

Inneres der Altneusynagoge, einer der bedeutendsten sakralen jüdischen Bauten in Europa, die im letzten Drittel des 13. Jahrhunderts entstand. Der zweischiffige Hallenraum bildet den Kern des Baus und ist ein Werk einer südböhmischen Zisterzienserbauhütte.
<

Die Hohe bzw. Rathaussynagoge ließ 1577 Mordechai Maisel errichten, ein märchenhaft reicher Bankier, eine bedeutende Persönlichkeit des Rudolfinischen Prags.

The interior of the Old-New (Staronová) Synagogue, one of the most outstanding Jewish sacral buildings in Europe, originated in the last third of the 13th century. The hall-type double nave forming the core of the building is the work of the South Bohemian Cistercian workshop.
<

The High (Vysoká) or Town Hall (Radniční) Synagogue was built on the impulse of Mordechai Maisel, a banker of fairy-tale wealth and a significant personality of Rudolphian Prague.

JUDENSTADT
Die jüdische Siedlung, deren Anfänge vielleicht bis in das 10. Jahrhundert zurückreichen, war ein eigenständiger Teil des Altstädter Wohnviertels. Zuletzt bildete sich eine jüdische Besiedlung im Raum nördlich des Altsädter Rings heraus, wo ein typisches mittelalterliches Ghetto entstand, trotz rechtsungleicher Bedingungen ein wichtiges Element im Leben der Stadt.

THE JEWISH TOWN
The Jewish community, whose beginnings perhaps fall in the 10th century, formed an individual and characteristic part of the population of the Old Town. Jewish settlement finally became stabilized on the area lying to the north of Old Town Square, where a typical medieval ghetto originated which formed an important element in the life of the town in spite of its unequal conditions.

JUDENSTADT
Der ausgedehnteste Rest der damaligen
Judenstadt ist der Alte jüdische
Friedhof, auf dem Grabmäler aus den
Jahren 1439–1787 zu finden sind.
Auf seinem Gebiet stehen zwei Synagogen –
die Klausen-Synagoge (rechts) von 1694,
heute eine der Expositionen des
Staatlichen jüdischen Museums und die
Pinkassynagoge, gegründet 1479 und
erweitert in der 1. Hälfte des 10. Jh.
An ihre Wände wurden die Namen von
77 297 jüdischen Opfern des
nazistischen Genozids geschrieben.

THE JEWISH TOWN
The biggest remainder of the former
Jewish Town is the Old Jewish Cemetery
containing gravestones from the
period of 1439 to 1787.
Two synagogues stand on its periphery –
the Klausen Synagogue (on the right)
of 1694, now containing one of the
expositions of the State Jewish Museum,
and the Pinkas Synagogue, founded
in 1479 and enlarged in the first half
of the 16th century. The names of
77, 297 Jewish victims of Nazi genocide
are inscribed on its walls.

Die Kleinseite ist ein architektonisches Kleinod mit einer ausgewogenen Proportion von Großzügigkeit des befangen machenden Materials und mikrografischen handwerklichen Details – Barocktor beim hl. Thomas.

>
Blick vom Kleinseitner Brückenturm auf einen Teil der Kleinseite und auf die Prager Burg.

The Little Quarter is an architectural gem with the well-balanced proportions of grandiosely conceived masses and a small craft detail – the Baroque portal of St. Thomas's Church.

>
View from the Little Quarter Bridge Tower of a part of the Little Quarter and Prague Castle.

KLEINSEITE

Die Kleinseite, die älteste Prager Ansiedlung unterhalb der Burg, wird seit der Zuerkennung des Stadtrechtes 1257 zunächst Neustadt bezeichnet, danach Kleinere Stadt. Seit Beginn ihrer Entstehung war sie eng mit dem Herrschaftssitz verbunden. Ihr heutiges Antlitz formte sich in einem malerischen, dafür allerdings überwiegend abschüssigem Terrain. Im Unterschied zur Altstadt befand sich hier keine dichte Ansammlung sakraler Bauten. Dafür aber siedelten hier gegen Ende des 12. bis zum Beginn des 15. Jahrhunderts in weitläufigen befestigten Residenzen Prager Bischöfe und Erzbischöfe. Nach dem Brand von 1541 begann die Kleinseite, sich in ein Residenzviertel zu verwandeln. Die baulichen Veränderungen und die Errichtung neuer Klöster und vor allem der Neubau der St.-Nikolaus-Kirche waren vom Barock geprägt.

THE LITTLE QUARTER

The Little Quarter, Prague's oldest outer bailey, first called the New and later the Lesser Town from the time of its raising to a town, was closely connected with the seat of the ruler from the moment of its origin. It developed into its present form in picturesque, but mostly hilly terrain running into a narrow level strip by the bank of the Vltava. Contrary to the Old Town, there was not such a dense concentration of sacral buildings here. On the other hand, however, Prague's bishops and archbishops resided here in big, fortified residences from the end of the 12th to the beginning of the 15th century. After the great fire of 1541 the Little Quarter began to change into a residential quarter. The Baroque crowned this transformation with the origin of new monastery areas and in particular with the new building of St. Nicholas's Church.

ST. NIKOLAUS

Dreischiffige Pfarrkirche aus dem 13. Jahrhundert,
seit 1628 Teil des Jesuitenkollegs, wurde durch
den Neubau der heutigen Kirche in drei Phasen ersetzt.
In der ersten 1704–11 errichtete Christoph
Dientzenhofer das Schiff und die Westfassade.
Der Sohn, Kilian Ignaz, projektierte den Abschluß mit
der Kuppel (1737–52) und Anselmo Lurago
errichtete 1751–56 den Glockenturm.
Die Ausgestaltung mit Plastiken ist überwiegend
ein Werk von I. F. Platzer, die Fresken stammen
von J. L. Kracker und F. X. Balko. Hervorragende
Orgel von 1746.

ST. NICHOLAS'S CHURCH

A triple-naved parish church of the 13th century,
from 1628 a part of the college of the Jesuits, which
was replaced with the new building of the present
church in three phases. Between 1704 and 1711
Kryštof Dientzenhofer built the nave and the western
façade. His son, Kilian I. Dientzenhofer, designed the
east end with a dome (1737–1752) and Anselmo Lurago
built the belfry in the years 1751 to 1756.
The sculptural decoration is mainly the work
of I. F. Platzer, while the frescoes were painted
by J. L. Kracker and F. X. Balko. The excellent
organ dates from 1746.

Der Blick vom Laurenziberg auf die Kirche des hl. Nikolaus und das Jesuitenkolleg zeigt die neue Dimension der barocken Monumentalität im mikrografischen mittelalterlichen Urbanismus.

Das Interieur ist ein Zusammenspiel der schwelgenden Form, des Spiels des Lichtes und der wirkungsvollen Kombination unterschiedlich farbiger Materialien. Im Vordergrund eine Kanzel aus den sechziger Jahren des 18. Jahrhunderts.

The view from Petřín of St. Nicholas's Church and the Jesuit college shows the new dimension of Baroque monumentality amid the small-scale architecture of medieval urbanism.

The interior of the choir, abounding in diverse shapes, a play of light and an effective combination of variously coloured materials. In the foreground: the pulpit, dating from the 1760's.

ST. THOMAS

Im Jahre 1285 wurde das Kloster der Augustiner-Eremiten mit der Kirche St. Thomas gegründet. Die Kirche wurde mehrmals umgebaut, zuletzt durch K. I. Dientzenhofer von 1723–31, V. V. Reiner gestaltete sie mit Deckenfresken aus. Das Mobiliar ist zeitgenössisch entsprechend dem Umbau, es finden sich aber auch wertvolle Stücke aus der ehemaligen Kirche. Der Hauptaltar mit Gemälden von P. P. Rubens wurde von K. I. Dientzenhofer entworfen (Originale in der Nationalgalerie).

ST. THOMAS'S CHURCH

The monastery of the order of Augustinians-Hermits was founded with St. Thomas's Church in 1285. The church was rebuilt several times, its last reconstruction being carried out by K. I. Dientzenhofer between 1723 and 1731. The ceiling frescoes are the work of V. V. Reiner. The movables date from the same period as the reconstruction, but they also include a number of valuable works from the time preceding it. The high altar with paintings by P. P. Rubens was designed by K. I. Dientzenhofer (the originals are housed in the National Gallery).

ST. THOMAS

Das Augustinerkloster bei
der St.-Thomas-Kirche gehörte zu den
reichsten und einflußreichsten.
Neben einem eigenen Konvent gehörte ein
ausgedehntes Hinterland zu ihm, einschließlich
einer 1358 gegründeten Bierbrauerei.
Trotz einer Reihe von Umbauten bewahrte sich
die St.-Thomas-Kirche in der Disposition
der Höheneinteilung den ursprünglichen
Charakter einer mendikantischen Basilika mit
durchgehendem Chor, außerdem kommt
die gesamte Konfiguration der Kleinseite
zur Geltung.

ST. THOMAS'S CHURCH

The Augustinian monastery attached to
St. Thomas's Church ranked among the richest
and the most influential. Apart from the
convent proper, extensive property in the
environs, including a brewery founded in 1358,
belonged to it. In spite of the number
of reconstructions to which it was subjected
St. Thomas's Church preserved in its
ground-plan and height conception its original
character of a mendicant basilica with an
elongated chancel, being a striking landmark
in the general configuration
of the Little Quarter.

ST. JOSEF

In die bunte Komposition von Bautypen
und Stilnuancen des Prager Barocks bringt
der Karmeliter Donatus Ignacius à Jesùs
in eigenwilliger Weise etwas Besonderes ein.
Der ovale Zentralraum der Kirche ist mit einer
reich gegliederten plastischen Fassade
ausgestattet, die niederländischen Einfluß
verrät. Die Kirche wurde 1686–92 errichtet.
Hinter ihrer nicht großen, in der Straßenflucht
zurücktretenden Fassade breitet sich
das eigentliche Kloster mit einem ausgedehnten
Garten aus, den heutigen Vojan-Gärten.

ST. JOSEPH'S CHURCH

A contribution to the wide variety
of architectural types and nuances of style of
the Prague Baroque was made by the Carmelite
monk Donatus Ignacius à Jesù.
The oval central part of the church has
a richly sculpturally decorated façade,
betraying Netherlandish orientation.
The church was built from 1686 to 1692.
Its own monastery with a large garden,
now Vojan Park, stood beyond its façade,
which, fairly small in size, projects
from the street line.

Das Paar massiver Türme, das den Kirchenvorraum zusammenfaßt, ist ein Überrest des hochgotischen Umbaus der Kirche der Jungfrau Maria nach 1370, es ruft den Eindruck eines befestigten Sitzes der Ritterkommende hervor.

>

Überreste von Arkaden der ursprünglichen Konventkirche - einer Basilika aus den Jahren 1158-82 im Raum zwischen dem Vorsaal und dem erhalten gebliebenden Torso der gotischen Kirche.

The massive twin towers on the sides of the vestibule of the Church of Our Lady Below the Chain, remainders of the High Gothic reconstruction of the building after 1370, evoke the character of the fortified seat of a community of knights.

>

Remnants of the arcades of the original convent church – a basilica (1158–1182) in the space between the vestibule and the preserved torso of the Gothic church.

JUNGFRAU MARIA UNTER DER KETTE

Als Reaktion auf die Kreuzzüge wurde ein heimischer Zweig der Ritterorden gegründet. 1158 gründete Kanzler Gervasius unter Beistand von König Wladislaw I., der selbst am Barbarossa-Zug teilgenommen hatte, am Kleinseitner Ufer die Kommende der Johanniter zur Jungfrau Maria, genannt nach dem Platz am Ende der Brücke.

THE CHURCH OF OUR LADY BELOW THE CHAIN

One of the results of the Crusades was the formation of domestic branches of various orders of knights. In 1158 Chancellor Gervasius founded, with the help of King Vladislav I, who himself took part in Barbarossa's crusade, the monastery of Maltese Knights on the Little Quarter bank of the River Vltava. Due to its position it was called The End of the Bridge.

JUNGFRAU MARIA UNTER DER KETTE

Die Johanniter nahmen das ausgedehnte Gebiet zwischen der Moldau und der Karmeliterstraße am strategisch wichtigen Brückenkopf in Besitz, das über die Brückenstraße an den nicht erhaltenen, ebenfalls befestigten, ausgedehnten Bischofssitz angrenzte. Die heutige Kirche ist eigentlich das barockisierte Presbyterium der frühgotischen Kirche. Ein Gemälde von Karel Škréta, entstanden um 1650, schmückt den Altar, das die Feier zur siegreichen Schlacht bei Lepanto und des Malteserordens darstellt.

THE CHURCH OF OUR LADY BELOW THE CHAIN

The Maltese Knights occupied the large territory between the River Vltava and Karmelitská Street on the strategically important bridgehead, neighbouring via Mostecká Street with the unpreserved big, fortified seat of the bishop. The present church consists of the Barocized presbytery of an Early Gothic church. The high altar is decorated with a painting by Karel Škréta (c. 1650). It celebrates the Battle of Lepanto and the Maltese Order.

Blick von den Gärten des Laurenziberges auf der Kleinseite, im Vordergrund die Kirche der siegreichen Jungfrau Maria.

>

Das frühbarocke Portal der Kirche in der Karmeliterstraße

View from Petřín Park of the Little Quarter with the Church of Our Lady Victorious in the foreground.

>

The Early Baroque portal of the church from Karmelitská Street.

PRAGER JESUSKIND
Nach der Niederlage der Ständeerhebung in der Schlacht auf dem Weißen Berg wurde den deutschen Lutheranern die erst neu errichtete Dreifaltigkeits-Kirche abgenommen und den Karmelitern zugesprochen. Sie richteten ihr Glaubensleben in westlicher Orientierung aus und weihten die Kirche der siegreichen Jungfrau Maria. Die zweite ihr ebenfalls geweihte Kirche wurde auf dem Weißen Berg errichtet.

THE PRAGUE CHILD JESUS
After the defeat of the uprising of the Estates in the Battle of the White Mountain in 1620 the Church of the Holiest Trinity of the German Lutherans, built a short time previously, was taken from them and handed over to the Carmelites, who newly oriented it in westerly direction and consecrated it to Our Lady Victorious. Another church consecrated to Our Lady Victorious was built on the White Mountain (Bílá hora).

Weltruhm und Beliebtheit
bei den Pilgern, vor allem bei den
iberoamerikanischen, erwarb sich
die Kirche der siegreichen Jungfrau
Maria durch ein kleines Denkmal -
das Prager Jesuskind.

World renown and popularity among
pilgrims, especially Iberian-American
ones, was gained for the Church
of Our Lady Victorious by a small
monument in the form of the Prague
Child Jesus.

Altar des Prager
Jesuskindes,
befindet sich in einer
flachen Nische der
Nordwand der
Saalkirche. Er wurde
1776 errichtet.

>
Polyxena von
Lobkowicz widmete
1628 der Kirche die
Wachsfigur des
Jesuskindes, eine
spanische Arbeit
Mitte des 16. Jh. Das
Jesuskind wurde
innerhalb kurzer Zeit
zum Gegenstand der
Adoration, und zu
ihm gehört eine
große Sammlung
von Gewändern, die
Gläubige widmeten.

The altar of the
Prague Child Jesus,
founded in 1776,
stands in a shallow
niche in the northern
wall of the hall-type
church.

>
The wax statue of
the Child Jesus, a
Spanish work of the
mid-16th century,
was presented to the
church by Polyxena
of Lobkowicz in 1628.
In a short space of
time the Child Jesus
became an object of
adoration and in the
course of the years
believers have
supplied the statue
with a large
collection of
valuable garments.

ST. JOHANN AN DER WÄSCHE
Ebenso wie die übrigen Prager
Städte wuchs die Kleinseite so,
daß sie neben ihrem Kern
auch umgebende frühere
Siedlungen einbezog.
Die Johanneskirche wurde schon 1142
als Pfarrkirche des Dorfes
Újezd erwähnt. Nach 1235 erfolgte
der frühgotische Umbau.
Sie bildet mit dem benachbarten
Kleinseitner Hospital (gegr. 1662)
ein malerisches Ganzes.

THE CHURCH OF ST. JOHN AT THE LAUNDRY
Similarly as the other towns
of Prague, the Little Quarter
originated as its part on an open
space into which older communities
and courts were incorporated.
The John's at the Laundry
was the parish church of the
community Újezd already in 1142.
After 1235 it was rebuilt in Early
Gothic style. It forms a picturesque
whole with the neighbouring Little
Quarter hospital, founded in 1662.

Kleinseite | The Little Quarter

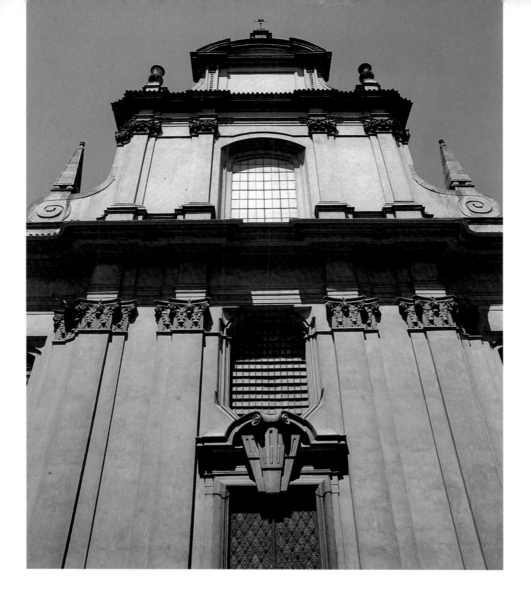

THEATINER-FRAUENKIRCHE
Zur Entwicklung des frühen Prager
Barocks leisteten neben einheimischen
Meistern und zahlreichen Einwanderern
auch seltene Projektimporte
einen Beitrag.
So zeichnete Guarino Guarini 1679
sein elegantes Projekt
für die Theatiner Klosterkirche.
Sein Entwurf wurde jedoch durch ein
Projekt von J. B. Matthey und J. Santini
ersetzt (1691–1771 erbaut).

THE CHURCH OF OUR LADY AT THE THEATINS
Apart from the work of architects and builders
who had settled in Bohemia, it was particularly
Italians and the occasional import of projects
that represented the impulses of the new style -
the Early Baroque. In 1679, for example,
Guarino Guarini designed the monastery Church
of the Theatins in Nerudova Street. Its boldly
designed, dynamic interior was not realized,
the church finally being built from 1691
to 1711 after a design by J. B. Matthey
and J. B. Santini.

Geißelung Christi
und Pilatus – Details
aus dem
Passionszyklus im
unteren Streifen von
Malereien in der
St.-Wenzels-Kapelle.
1372.

>
Blick von der
Terrasse der
Reitschule der
Prager Burg über
den Hirschgraben
auf die
St.-Veits-Kathedrale
von Norden.

The Whipping of
Christ and Pilate –
details from the
Passion cycle in the
lower band of
paintings in St.
Wenceslas's Chapel
(1372).

>
View from the
terrace of the
Riding-school of
Prague Castle across
Stag Moat to St.
Vitus's Cathedral
(seen from the north).

PRAGER BURG | PRAGUE CASTLE

Die Prager Burg stellt zusammen mit
dem Städtchen Hradčany und dem
Strahov-Kloster ein herrliches
Diadem der Stadt dar. Sie war Sitz
weltlicher und geistlicher Mächte und
gleichzeitig Stätte der
Stammeszusammenkünfte, später der
Landtagsversammlungen. Von Anbeginn bildete die St.-Veits-Kirche
das geistige Zentrum der Stadt wie
des Landes. Neben Zeremonien wie
sie die Folge des Kirchenjahres
wiederholt brachte fanden hier auch
die Krönungen böhmischer Könige
statt, deren irdisches Dasein in
der hiesigen Königsgruft beschlossen
wurde. Aber auch die anderen Kirchen besaßen ihren festen Platz und
ihre Bedeutung im Leben des Landes.
Sie geben Auskunft über die
schöpferischen Spannungen und be-
wegten Momente der Geschichte, sie
verkörpern Legenden und Mythen
ebenso wie Tatsachen des Lebens.

Together with the township of
Hradčany and the monastery on
Strahov Prague Castle forms the magnificent diadem of the city. It was the
seat of secular and sacral power and
also the scene of tribal gatherings and
later of the provincial Diets.
St. Vitus's Cathedral was the
spiritual centre of the town and the
country from the very beginning.
Rites dictated by the order of the
church year repeatedly took place
here and the cathedral was the setting
for the coronation of Czech kings,
whose earthly pilgrimage ended in
the royal tomb in the building. From
the Middle Ages other churches also
had their own firm place and importance in the life of the country. They
bear witness to the creative endeavours and moving moments
which marked the history of the
country and embody legends, myths
and simple facts of life.

Blick durch die Kathedrale vom Chor nach Westen. Im Vordergrund das marmorne Königsmausoleum, ein Werk des niederländischen Bildhauers Alexander Collin aus den Jahren 1571-1589, errichtet für Ferdinand I., dessen Gattin Anna Jagiello und deren Sohn Maxmilian II, deren Gestalten in die Deckplatte der Marmortumba eingemeiselt wurden. Das Rosettenfenster an der westlichen neugotischen Fassade wurde von F. Kysela von 1921-27 geschaffen. Es zeigt Motive der Erschaffung der Welt.

>
St. VEIT
Dem Wirken von Kamil Hilbert, dem Hauptarchitekten der Baubeendigung der Kathedrale, ist die beachtenswerte Abkehr vom Pseudostil des Purismus und der Hinwendung zur zeitgenössischen bildenden Kunst und dem Kunsthandwerk zu verdanken. Das trug auch zur Erneuerung der tschechischen Vitrage bei. An der Ausgestaltung des neuen Teils der Kathedrale war auch Alfons Mucha mit einem Fenster der erzbischöflichen Kapelle beteiligt, das die älteste christliche Tradition, beginnend mit Cyrill und Methodius, darstellt.

Von Beginn an bildete die St.-Veits-Kirche den Ort der Landeshauptkirche und erfüllte die Funktion einer Pfarr-, Kolleg- und Kathedralkirche sowie die Aufgabe eines Ortes staatlicher Zeremonien. Ihre ältesten Teile, die St.-Veits-Rotunde und die Basilika aus der 2. Hälfte des 11. Jahrhunderts führen uns archäologische Funde aus den unterirdischen Teilen der Kathedrale vor Augen.

From the very beginning St. Vitus's Church was the principal church of the country, fulfilling the function of the parish, collegiate and cathedral church and the role of the state and ceremonial church. An idea of its two oldest forms, Václav's rotunda and the basilica of the mid-11th century, is afforded by archeological finds in the underground part of the cathedral and outside the building.

View through the cathedral from the chancel towards the west. In the foreground the marble royal mausoleum, the work of the Netherlandish sculptor Alexander Collin, built (1571-1589) for Ferdinand I, his consort Anne Jagello and their son Maxmilian II, whose figures are carved on the top slabs. The rosette window in the western, Neo-Gothic façade is the work of F. Kysela (1921-1927) after the motif The Creation of the World.

>
ST. VITUS'S CATHEDRAL
The activity of Kamil Hilbert as the chief architect responsible for the completion of the cathedral was marked by a significant decline away from pseudo-style purism to the application of contemporary creative art and the artistic craft. Apart from other things, it also led to the revival of Czech window glass. Alfons Mucha also contributed to the decoration of the new part of the cathedral with the window of the Archbishop's Chapel. It portrays the oldest Christian tradition beginning with SS. Cyril and Methodius.

St.-Veits-Kathedrale
von Südwesten.
Links das Gebäude
der alten Probstei, im
Kern des Gemäuers
der romanische
Palast der Prager
Bischöfe. Rechts
davon die
ausgegrabenen
Fundamente der
Bischofskapelle mit
dem östlichen Teil
der romanischen
Basilika.

>
Blick durch das
Hauptschiff der
Kathedrale nach
Osten.

View of St. Vitus's
Cathedral from the
south-west. Seen on
the left is the
building of the Old
Provost's Residence.
Masonry of the
Romanesque palace
of the bishops of
Prague has been
preserved in its core.
Situated on its right
are the roofed
excavations of the
foundations of the
Bishop's Chapel and
the western part of
the Romanesque
basilica.

>
View of the main
nave of the cathedral
towards the east.

ST. VEIT

Das großzügig angelegte Werk der
St.-Veits-Kathedrale blieb ein Torso,
wenn auch Peter Parler und nach ihm
dessen Söhne nach dem Tode ihres
Gründers Karl IV. im Werk fortsetzten.
Die hussitische Epoche bedeutete
Einstellung der Arbeit. Um die
Bauweiterführung bemühten sich 1509
König Wladislaw Jagiello und nach
ihm Kaiser Leopold II., der der
Weissagung Glauben schenkte, daß
derjenige die Kathedrale beendet,
der die Türken aus Europa vertreibt.

ST. VITUS'S CATHEDRAL

The grandly planned St. Vitus's Cathedral
remained a torso only even though after
the death of its founder, Charles IV,
its construction was continued
by Peter Parler and, after him, by his
sons. The Hussite epoch brought building
activity here to a halt. In 1509 King
Vladislav Jagello tried to complete
the work, followed in 1673 by the
Emperor Leopold II, inspired among
other things by the prophesy that the
person who completed the cathedral
would drive the Turks from Europe.

Südlicher Vorraum der Kathedrale, sog. Goldene Pforte mit einem Mosaik des Jüngsten Gerichts aus den Jahren 1570–71.

The southern vestibule of the cathedral, the so-called Golden Portal with a mosaic portraying The Last Judgement (1370–1371).

ST. VEIT

Bei der Errichtung des hohen Chors der Kathedrale stellte Peter Parler seine ausgereifte Meisterschaft unter Beweis. Die Bauten dazu begannen 1371. Die maximale Materialbeschränkung bei den Fensterwänden, verbunden mit vollem Hervorheben der Plastizität der architektonischen Teile und des Wellenrhythmus der unter den Fenstern befindlichen Simse über dem Triforium krönt das Muster des Netzgewölbes.

ST. VITUS'S CATHEDRAL

Peter Parler proved his mature virtuosity in the construction of the high chancel, built from 1371. The maximum degree of dematerialization of the window wall along with full application of the plasticity of the architectural elements and the undulating rhythm of the cornices below the windows above the triforium are crowned by the figure of the net vault.

Blick zum Chor, im Vordergrund
die frühbarocke Kanzel von 1618,
im Hintergrund die Kapelle
des hl. Sigismund mit Altar,
entworfen von Fischer von Erlach.

View of the chancel;
in the foreground the Early Baroque
pulpit of 1618, in the background
St. Sigismund's Chapel with an altar
designed by Fischer von Erlach.

ST. VEIT

Nach jahrhundertlanger Stagnation
der Bautätigkeit und Ausgestaltung
der Kathedrale bringt das Interesse
des Herrschers Wladislaw Jagiello,
katholischer König polnischen
Ursprungs, neue Belebung. Neben der
Erneuerung der Befestigungen und des
Königspalastes wurde die Kathedrale
1493 Ort des Aufmerksamkeit
erweckenden königlichen Oratoriums,
ein Werk von Hans Spiess
aus Frankfurt.

ST. VITUS'S CATHEDRAL

After almost one hundred years
of stagnation of the construction
and decoration of the cathedral
interest in these activities was
revived during the reign of Vladislav
Jagello, a Catholic king of Polish
origin. Apart from the restoration
of the fortifications and the royal
palace the cathedral was provided in
1493 with the remarkable royal oratory,
built by Hans Spiess
of Frankfurt.

Blick auf den Südteil des Stützsystems des Parlerschen Chors der Kathedrale.

View of the southern part of the supporting system of Peter Parler's chancel of St Vitus's Cathedral.

>
ST. VEIT
Ehrbezeigung und Traditionsbewußtsein Karls IV. spiegeln sich in der außergewöhnlichen baulichen Gestaltung der St.-Wenzels-Kapelle. Südfront mit der Figur des Heiligen (J. Parler, 1373), mit Malereien aus dem 14.-16. Jahrhundert.

>
ST. VITUS'S CATHEDRAL
Charles IV expressed his respect for and emphasis on the tradition of the provincial saint through the exceptional architectural character of St. Wenceslas's Chapel. The southern wall with a statue of the saint (J. Parler, 1373), decorated with paintings of the 14th to the 16th century.

ST. GEORG
Südportal der Basilika des hl. Georg,
bereits ein Renaissancewerk der Hütte
B. Rieds nach 1500 mit spätgotischem Relief
des Kampfes des Heiligen mit dem Drachen.

>
St.-Georgs-Basilika von Osten. Türmepaar
Mitte des 12. Jahrhunderts. Links
von der Hauptapsis die gotische Kapelle
der hl. Ludmilla, errichtet auf einer älteren
Substruktion der Kapelle gegen Ende
des 14. Jahrhunderts.

ST. GEORGE'S BASILICA
The southern portal of St. George's Basilica,
a Renaissance work of B. Ried's workshop built
after 1500, decorated with a Late Gothic relief
portraying the saint's battle with the dragon.

>
St. George's Basilica from the east. The twin
steeples are from the mid-12th century.
On the left of the main apse is the Gothic
chapel consecrated to St. Ludmila, built on
an older substructure of the chapel
in the late 14th century.

ST. GEORG
Der Evangelist Markus, Detail der Ausgestaltung
der Kapelle der hl. Ludmilla vor 1600.
Rechts – Blick in den Abschluß der St.-Georgs –
Basilika. Chor aus der Zeit nach der Mitte
des 12. Jahrhunderts mit Resten später
romanischer Gewölbemalereien. Vor dem zur
Empore führenden Barockgeländer wurden die
Přemyslidenherrscher des 10.–11. Jahrhunderts
beigesetzt, einschließlich Vratislav I.,
der Kirchengründer.

ST. GEORGE'S BASILICA
Mark the Evangelist, detail of the decoration
of St. Ludmila's Chapel (before 1600).
On the right – view of the east end of
St. George's Basilica and the chancel from
the mid-12th century with remainders of Late
Romanesque paintings on the vault.
The Přemyslid rulers of the 10th and 11th
centuries, beginning with Vratislav I, who
founded the church, are buried below the
Baroque balustrade leading to the choir.

Hofkapelle des hl. Kreuzes auf dem 2. Burghof der Prager Burg aus der Zeit nach der Mitte des 18. Jahrhunderts, klassizistische Gestaltung nach 1852. Heute ist hier die Exposition des Kirchenschatzes der St.-Veits-Kathedrale untergebracht.
<

The court Chapel of the Holy Rood in the Second Courtyard of Prague Castle. It originated after the mid-18th century and was modified in Classical style in 1852. An exposition of the treasure of St. Vitus's Cathedral is situated here.
<

ALLERHEILIGEN-KIRCHE

Kapitelkirche Allerheiligen, ursprüngliche Hofkapelle des Königs- und Fürstenpalastes, Přemysl Otakar II. ließ in der zweiten Hälfte des 13. Jh. die Kirche umbauen. Den Chor des heutigen Bauwerks errichtete 1370–78 Peter Parler nach dem Muster der Pariser St. Chapelle. Karl IV. richtete hier das Kapitel der Universitätsmeister ein. Nach dem Brand von 1541 wurde die Kirche erneuert und dreischiffig eingerichtet sowie mit dem Wladislaw-Saal verbunden.

ALL SAINTS CHURCH

The chapter Church of All Saints, originally the court chapel of the royal and prince's palace, in its oldest form as a part of the Romanesque palace of the 12th century. Přemysl Otakar II had the church built in the mid-13th century. The chancel of the present building was built from 1370 to 1378 by Peter Parler after the model of St. Chapelle in Paris. Charles IV founded the chapter of university masters here. After a fire which occurred in 1541 the church was repaired and a triple nave connected with the Vladislav Hall was built.

Vielgestaltigkeit der Kirchenarchitektur und des Formenreichtums sowie die Bauauffassungen wirkten in vielerlei Hinsicht inspirativ auf die Entwicklung des Bauwesens, der künstlerischen Fachbereiche und der Handwerke. Trotz der Mißgeschicke wie es Brände waren - erinnert sei an den Brand von Hradčany und der Kleinseite von 1541 -, die Bilderstürmerei in der Hussitenzeit von 1420 oder die Kalvinisten von 1619, Plünderungen durch ausländische Soldaten oder die Requisition von Edelmetallen durch die Herrscher-blieben sie unerschöpfliche Quellen der Erkenntnis und Inspiration.

In many respects the diversity of church architecture and the wealth of forms and approaches it represented had an inspiring influence on the development of building activity and the arts and crafts. In spite of disasters such as fires, brought to mind to the greatest extent by the catastrophic fire at Hradčany and in the Little Quarter in 1541, the image-breaking activities of the Hussites in 1420 and the Calvinists in 1619, the looting of churches by foreign troops and the requisition of precious metals by the rulers of the country they remained an inexhaustible source of knowledge and inspiration.

St.-Benedikts-Kirche auf dem Hradschiner Platz, ursprüngliche Pfarrkirche des Städtchens Hradschin, zweite Hälfte des 14. Jh. 1626-1778 dem Barnabiten-Orden angeschlossen. Die Barnabiter rekonstruierten die Kirche und richteten bei ihr ein Kloster ein. 1792-1950 siedelten hier die Karmeliterinnen.

>
Nordfront des Hradschiner Platzes, beherrscht von der ausladenden Fassade des erzbischöflichen Palastes, das an den Ehrenhof der Prager Burg anschließt.

St. Benedict's Church in Hradčanské Square, originally the parish church of the small town of Hradčany from the mid-14th century. From 1626 to 1778 it belonged to the Barnabite order, which modified it and founded a monastery next to it. From 1792 to 1950 the Carmelites had their seat here.

>
The northern front of Hradčanské Square is dominated by the large façade of the Archbishop's Palace, which adjoins the cour d'honneur of Prague Castle.

HRADSCHIN
Die Prager Bischöfe siedelten von Beginn an im Palast bei der St.-Veits-Kirche auf der Burg, vom 12. Jahrhundert an in einem ausgedehnten Hof auf der Kleinseite. Bei der Erneuerung des Erzbistums 1562 wählten sie ihren Sitz auf dem Hradschiner Platz, in einem Gebäude, schrittweise hergerichtet, das 1675-79 durch J. B. Matthey zu einem frühbarocken Palast umgebaut wurde, 1764-65 erhielt es die jetzige Fassade, die den Palastkern in die Form zweier Risaliten erweitert.

HRADČANY
From the beginning the bishops of Prague had their seat in the palace by St. Vitus's Church at Prague Castle, but later, from the 12th century, they moved to a large court in the Little Quarter. When the archdiocese was renewed in 1562 they settled in Hradčanské Square, occupying a house which underwent several modifications. From 1675 to 1679 J. B. Matthey converted it into an Early Baroque palace. From 1764 to 1765 the building acquired its present façade, enlarging the body of the palace sideways by means of two projections.

STRAHOV

Hoch über der Stadt zwischen den Erhebungen
Laurenziberg und Prager Burg liegt das
ausgedehnte Gelände des Strahov-Klosters.
Es wurde 1140 durch König Vladislav I. am
strategisch wichtigen westlichen Zugang zur
Stadt gegründet (Strahov - abgel.
von Wachhügel). Die Prämonstrater
errichteten bis 1182 hier die Mariä-
Himmelfahrts-Kirche und den Kern des Konvents-
Gebäudes, bis heute in den Gemäuern erhalten.
Im 13. Jahrhundert wurde eine Kirche mit
gotischen Gewölben eingerichtet.

STRAHOV

Situated high above the town, between the
summit of Petřín and Prague Castle,
is the large area of Strahov Monastery. It was
founded in 1140 by King Vladislav I
on the strategically important western approach
to the town (Strahov = watch hill).
Until 1182 the Premonstrates built
the Basilica of the Assumption of Our Lady
and the core of the convent buildings,
still preserved in its masonry, here.
In the 13th century the church was
provided with Gothic vaults.

Prager Burg | Prague Castle

STRAHOV

Die kulturelle Entwicklung des Klosters gipfelte im 18. Jh., als das gesamte Gelände zu seiner heutigen Gestalt - einschließlich der künstlerischen Ausgestaltung - umgebaut wurde. Damals wurde die ausgezeichnete Klosterbibliothek eingerichtet, deren Philosophischer Saal 1794 durch F. A. Maulbertsch mit Deckenmalereien ausgestaltet wurde. Die große Orgel in der Abteikirche von 1746 bewunderte auch Mozart und spielte selbstverständlich auf ihr. In einem Teil der Anlage ist die Gedenkstätte des Nationalen Schrifttums untergebracht - ein Literaturmuseum und Archiv.

STRAHOV

The cultural development of the monastery culminated in the 18th century, when the whole area was lent its present appearance, including the artistic decorations. In the same period the outstanding monastery library was newly adapted. In 1794 its Philosophical Hall was decorated with wall paintings by F. A. Maulbertsch. The big organ of 1746 in the abbey church was played by W. A. Mozart, who greatly admired it. The Museum of National Literature is situated in the monastery area.

LORETO

Das Loreto-Heiligtum, eine der Prager Barockschönheiten, wurde 1626 von Benigna Katherina von Lobkowicz gegründet. Dessen Kern bildet eine Kopie der Kapelle im italienischen Loreto, dem angeblichen Haus der Jungfrau Maria, das Engel von Nazareth hierher gebracht haben sollen. Das gesamte Gelände des Loreto, das die Christi-Geburts-Kirche und das Ambit einschließt, umgeben von einem ausgedehnten Hof, wuchs nach mehr als einem Jahrhundert empor. In bedeutender Weise waren die beiden Dientzenhofers mit Projekten am Aufbau beteiligt.

THE LORETTO

The Loretto, one of the attributes of Baroque Prague, was founded in 1626 by Benigna Kateřina of Lobkowicz. The core of the building is a copy of the chapel in the Italian Loretto, alleged to be the dwelling of the Virgin Mary, transferred here by angels from Nazareth. The whole area of the Loretto, including the Church of the Nativity of Our Lord and the cloister surrounding a large court, developed for over one hundred years. Plans by the two Dientzenhofers played an important role in the process.

KAPUZINERKLOSTER
Das Kloster der Kapuziner mit der Kirche der
Jungfrau Maria von den Engeln auf dem Loreto-
Platz, 1. Hälfte des 17. Jahrhunderts.

>
Blick vom Hauptturm des Loreto nach Osten
nach Hradschin und der St.-Veits-Kirche.
In den Arkaden des Turms wurden die Glocken
eines berühmten Glockenspiels aufgehängt,
installiert 1694.

THE CAPUCHIN MONASTERY
The Capuchin monastery with the Church
of Our Lady Angelic in Loretánské Square.
First half of the 17th century.

>
View in easterly direction of Hradčany
and St. Vitus's Cathedral from the
steeple of the Loretto. Hanging in the arcades
of the steeple are the bells of the renowned
carillon, installed here in 1694.

Spitzenwerke barocker Malerei, in reich profilierte Altararchitekturen eingefügt. St.-Ursula-Kirche.

>
Blick vom Wischehrad auf die Neustadt, rechts der Konvent der Elisabethanerinnen, links Emmaus-Kloster, im Vordergrund St. Johannes am Felsen.

Works of Baroque painting set in richly profiled altar structures in St. Ursula's Church.

>
View from Vyšehrad of the New Town. On the right the convent of the Elizabethan order, on the left the "Na Slovanech" (Emmaus) Monastery and in the centre the Church of St. John on the Rock.

NEUSTADT | THE NEW TOWN

Die Prager Neustadt wurde 1348 durch Karl IV. in einem weiten Bogen entlang der Altstädter Stadtmauer gegründet. Die großzügige urbanistische Konzeption verband Symbolik und Funktionalität in der Grundrißkomposition und der Festlegung von Dominanten, sie respektierte das vorhandene Netz der Hauptwege und einschließlich der verstreut liegenden Gehöfte. Zu den alten Heiligtümern kamen zwei neue Pfarrkirchen hinzu – die Stephans-Kirche und Heinrichs Kirche. Karl IV. gründete in der Neustadt sechs neue Klöster, die er mit Konventen jener Orden besetzte, die bislang im Land noch nicht wirkten.
In der Neustadt war nach weiteren fünfhundert Jahren ausreichend freie Fläche, und so fand der Barock hinlänglich Gelegenheiten für das kolossale Jesuitenkolleg auf dem Karlsplatz mit den der Straßenfront angepaßten Fassaden, sowie für weitere Neubauten.

Charles IV founded the New Town of Prague in 1348 in a wide bend along the Old Town fortifications. The grand-scale urban conception of the town combined symbolism and function in both the ground-plan composition and the location of the dominant features and respected the preserved network of main communications and, even if scattered, numerous communities. The oldest churches were joined by two new parish churches – St. Stephen's and St. Henry's. Charles IV founded six new monasteries in the New Town, making them available to orders which had previously not worked in the country.
After the elapse of the next five hundred years there was still an adequate amount of free space in the New Town and so the Baroque was able to build the colossal massif of the Jesuit college in Karlovo (Charles) Square and impressive façades sensitively composed in the street fronts.

Die
Maria-Schnee-Kirche
wurde zusammen mit
dem
Karmeliterkloster
durch Karl IV. im
Jahre 1347
gegründet. Bis zur
hussitischen Zeit, als
hier der radikale
Prediger Jan Želivský
predigte, wurde
lediglich das
Presbyterium
errichtet. 1606
nahmen die
Franziskaner die
Kirche in
Besitz.

The Church of Our
Lady of the Snows
was founded in 1347
by Charles IV along
with the monastery
of the Carmelites.
Up to the Hussite
period, when the
radical
Jan Želivský
preached here,
only the presbytery
had been built. In
1606 the deserted
church was taken
over by the
Franciscans.

Portal des
ehemaligen
Klosterfriedhofs bei
der
Maria-Schnee-Kirche.
Vierziger Jahre des
14. Jahrhunderts.

>

Dominante des
Inneren der
Maria-Schnee-Kirche
ist ein äußerst
großer, sehr
zeitlicher Altar von
1649–51., die größte
Altararchitektur des
böhmischen Barocks.

The portal of the
former monastery
graveyard at the
Church of Our Lady
of the Snows
(1340's).

>

The dominant
feature of the interior
of the Church of Our
Lady of the Snows is
the big, very early
altar of 1649 to
1651. It is the
biggest altar
structure of the
Czech Baroque.

Hauptaltar mit dem
Bildnis der Patronin
der
St.-Ursula-Kirche
von K. Liška von
1709.

>

Das durchleuchtete
Kircheninnere mit
der reichen Stuck-
und
Marmorgestaltung
der Wände.
Deckenfresko von J.
J. Steinfels von 1707.

The high altar with a
painting of the
patron saint of St.
Ursula's Church, the
work of K. Liška
(1709).

>

The illuminated
interior of the church
with rich stucco and
marble decorations
on the walls. The
ceiling frescoes by J.
J. Steinfels date from
1707.

ST. URSULA

Das Ursulinerinnenkloster
in der heutigen Nationalstraße
wurde 1672 gegründet.
Die Klosterkirche errichtete
M. A. Canevale von 1699–1704 als
hochbarocken Saal-Raum.
Ungewöhnlich ist die Lösung
des Eintritts von Norden,
in die Straßenfront,
den als Hauptein-
gang begriffenen Zugang.

ST. URSULA'S CHURCH

The convent of the Ursuline order
in present-day Národní Street
was founded in 1672. The convent
church consecrated to St. Ursula was
built by M. A. Canevale from 1699
to 1704 as a High Baroque, hall-type
structure. The entrance from
the northern façade, conceived
as the main one and set
in the street front,
is of an unusual design.

St. PETER

St.-Peter-Kirche von Poříčí, im Kern eine romanische dreischiffige Basilika, teilweise im 14. Jahrhundert umgebaut. Der leicht aufstrebende Glockenturm von 1598.

<

Die St.-Heinrich-Kirche wurde in der zweiten Hälfte des 14. Jahrhunderts für den unteren Teil der neu gegründeten Neustadt als Pfarrkirche errichtet.

ST. PETER'S CHURCH

St. Peter's Church "Na poříčí", originally a Romanesque basilica with three aisles, was partly reconstructed during the 14th century. The separate belfry dates from 1598.

<

St. Henry's Church was built as a parish church in the latter half of the 14th century for the lower part of the newly founded New Town.

ST. PETER

Rings um die St.-Peter-Kirche breitete sich seit Ende des 11. bis zum Beginn des 13. Jahrhunderts eine Ansiedlung deutscher Kaufleute aus, die unter dem direkten herrschaftlichen Schutz standen, ähnlich wie die Ansiedlungen der jüdischen und weiterer fremder Kaufleutekommunitäten. 1215 traten die deutschen Kaufleute die Kirche dem Orden der deutschen Ritter ab, sie wurden 1235 durch die Spitalbrüderschaft der hl. Agnes, später durch den Kreuzritterorden abgelöst. Seit 1252 Pfarrkirche.

ST. PETER'S CHURCH

From the late 11th to the early 13th century a community of German merchants, enjoying direct protection of the ruler similarly as settlements of Jewish and other foreign merchants, spread out round St. Peter's Church. In 1215 the German merchants placed the church at the disposal of the order of German Knights, whose place was taken in 1235 by the hospital brotherhood of St. Agnes and later by the order of the Knights of the Cross. Since 1252 the local parish church.

Gedenkplatte für die tschechoslowakischen Fallschirmspringer, die im Juni 1942 das Attentat auf Reichsprotektor R. Heydrich verübten, und die rechtgläubigen Priester, die sich für drei Wochen hier versteckt hielten. Die Fallschirmspringer wählten nach vergeblichem Widerstand gegen die nazistische Übermacht den Freitod.

>
Äußeres der St.-Karl-Borromäus-Kirche mit anliegendem Ruhestandshaus.

A tablet commemorating the Czechoslovak parachutists who, in June 1942, assassinated the Reichsprotektor R. Heydrich, and the orthodox priests who hid them in the church for three weeks. After trying in vain to resist superior Nazi forces, the parachutists chose death.

>
The exterior of the Church of St. Charles Borromaeus with the adjoining institute building.

ST. KARL BORROMÄUS
Emeritenhaus für bejahrte Priester, erbaut in den 30er Jahren des 18. Jahrhunderts. P. I. Bayer, beendet durch K. I. Dientzenhofer. Die Anstalt wurde 1783 aufgehoben und in eine Kaserne verwandelt. Ab 1866 dient es der Technischen Hochschule. Die Kirche dient seit 1935 der tschechoslowakischen rechtgläubigen Kirche unter der Weihe von St. Cyrill und Methodius.

THE CHURCH OF ST. CHARLES BORROMAEUS
The institute for emeritus priests was built in the thirties of the 18th century by P. I. Bayer, the work being finished by K. I. Dientzenhofer. In 1783 the institute was abolished and converted into barracks. Since 1866 it has served the needs of the Czech Technical University. Since 1935 the church has served the Czechoslovak Orthodox faith under the consecration SS. Cyril and Methodius.

Ähnlich wie in den beiden übrigen Prager Stadtgebieten nahmen die Jesuiten auch in der Neustadt ausgedehnte Grundstücke in Besitz, auf denen sie ab 1665 das Kolleg mit der St.-Ignacius-Kirche errichteten, deren monumentale Fassade ein Viertel des gesamten Karlsplatzes einnimmt. Eine Kirche mit typischer jesuitischer Disposition mit einzelnen gerahmten Kapellen und Tribünen über ihnen. Die reiche Innenausstattung des Kirchenraumes entstand nach einem ganzen Jahrhundert bis 1773, als das Kloster aufgehoben wurde und Josef II. die Jesuiten des Landes verwies. Das Kolleggelände wurde in ein Krankenhaus verwandelt.

Similarly as in the other two towns of Prague, large plots of land were owned by the Jesuits also in the New Town. From 1665 they built a college with St. Ignatius's Church on them. The monumental façades of these buildings take up a whole quarter of Karlovo Square. The church has the typical Jesuit ground-plan with one nave with frame chapels and tribunes above them. The rich decoration of the interior of the building originated throughout a whole century up to 1773, when the monastery was abolished and the Jesuits were banished from the country by Joseph II. The college was converted into a hospital.

Die dem hl. Stephan geweihte Pfarrkirche der oberen Neustadt wurde durch Karl IV. 1351 gegründet und 1401 baulich beendet. Im Inneren ist eine steinerne Kanzel aus der 1. Hälfte des 14. Jh. erhalten geblieben, außerdem ein Zinntaufbecken von 1462 und ein Tafelbild der Jungfrau Maria vom hl. Stephan aus dem Jahre 1472, das übrige Mobiliar ist in der Mehrheit frühbarock mit wertvollen Gemälden.

The parish church of the upper New Town, consecrated to St. Stephen, was founded by Charles IV in 1351, its construction being completed in 1401. A stone pulpit from the first half of the 14th century, a tin font of 1462 and a panel painting of the St. Stephen Madonna of 1472 have been preserved in the interior of the church. The other movables are mainly Early Baroque with valuable paintings.

>
In der Umgebung des heutigen hl. Stephan baute seit dem 10. Jh. die Siedlung Rybníček. Deren Pfarrkirche stammt vom Beginn des 12. Jahrhunderts, eine dem hl. Longinus geweihte romanische Rotunde, nachdem deren Patrozinium auf die Pfarrkirche Karls IV. übertragen wurde.

>
From the 10th century the community Rybníček was situated in the environs of St. Stephen's Church of the present. Its parish church, a Romanesque rotunda consecrated to St. Longinus after its original patrocinium had been transferred to Charles IV's parish church, dates from the early 12th century.

Das Kloster Na Slovanech oder Emmaus-Kloster wurde 1347 durch Karl IV. für die Benediktiner gegründet, die ihre Lithurgie in altslawischer Sprache ausübten. Im 15. Jahrhundert befand sich hier nur ein einziger calixtinischer Konvent. Die dreischiffige Hallenkirche wurde 1372 geweiht. Nach einem Luftangriff der Alliierten im Februar 1945 brannten Kloster und Kirche aus und wurden nach dem Krieg schrittweise erneuert.

The Monastery "Na Slovanech" (Emmaus) was founded by Charles IV in 1347 for the Benedictine order performing the liturgy in the Old Slavonic language. In the 15th century the only Utraquist convent was situated here. The hall-type, triple-naved Church of Our Lady was consecrated in 1372. In February 1945 the monastery and the church were destroyed by fire after an air raid carried out by the Allies, but after the war the buildings were gradually renewed.

Das Kloster war zu Zeiten Karls IV. ein Zentrum der Bildung und der Künste. Hier wirkte auch das bedeutende Skriptorium, vor 1360 schuf ein unbekannter Meister einen Zyklus von Wandmalereien in allen Winkeln des Ambits (die Abbildung zeigt die Szene der den Holofern beschattenden Judith). Zahlreiche Tafelgemälde schmücken die Kirche (Kreuzigung um 1360, heute in der Nationalgalerie).

At Charles IV's time the monastery was a centre of education and art culture with an important scriptorium. Before 1360 an unknown master painted a cycle of wall paintings in all branches of the cloister (the photo shows a detail of the scene portraying Judith executing Holofern). The church was decorated with numerous panel paintings on the Crucifixion theme (c. 1360), now housed in the National Gallery.

In den dreißiger Jahren des 18. Jh. errichtete K. I. Dientzenhofer in der Nachbarschaft des Emmaus-Klosters unter Ausnutzung des effektvollen Geländes die kleine, aber monumental wirkende Kirche des hl. Johannes von Nepomuk am Felsen. Sie besitzt eine dynamisch wirkende Fassade mit deutlicher Schrägstellung beider Türme.

In the thirties of the 18th century K. I. Dientzenhofer built the small, but monumentally conceived Church of St. John Nepomuk on the Rock, making effective use of the terrain in the neighbourhood of the Emmaus monastery. The building has a dynamically designed façade emphasized with obliquely built twin towers.

Die St.-Appollinarius-Kirche wurde durch Karl IV. gegründet, als 1362 das altertümliche Kapitel aus Sadská in die Neustadt übertragen wurde. Es handelt sich um eine einfache, einschiffige Kirche mit langgezogenem Presbyterium und einem Fassadenturm.

St. Apollinarius's Church was founded by Charles IV in 1362 when he transferred the old chapter from Sadská to the New Town. It is a simple, single-naved building with an elongated presbytery and a façade steeple.

Eine der Dominanten der Neustadt ist die Kirche der Jungfrau Maria und Karls des Großen am Karlshof, ebenfalls durch Karl IV. gegründet. Zu Zeiten Karls wurden die Mauern errichtet und das Dach provisorisch gedeckt. Das spätgotische Gewölbe wurde bis 1575 beendet. Die reiche barocke Innenausgestaltung besitzt die einheitliche Handschrift des Projekts von F. M. Kaňka von 1733.

The landmarks of the New Town include the Church of Our Lady and Charlemagne, also founded by Charles IV for the Augustinian canons. The peripheral walls and a provisionary roof were built during Charles's lifetime. The Late Gothic vault was not completed until 1575. The rich Baroque decorations and furnishings of the interior of the church have a uniform character given by F. M. Kaňka's design of 1733.

St. Katharina;
1355 gegründet
von Karl IV. als
Konventkirche des
Augustinianerinne-
klosters. Vom
prächtigen Bau blieb
nur der ächteckige
Turm erhalten. Das
Langhaus baute
1737–41 F. M.
Kaňka. In der reichen
inneren Ausstattung
ragen die
Deckenfresken von
V. V. Reiner hervor.

St. Catharine's,
founded by
Charles IV as
the convent
church of the
Augustinian
monastery (1355).
The steeple is the
only preserved part
of the building.
The nave was built
by F. M. Kaňka in the
years 1737 to 1741
and provided with
magnificent decorations.
On the vault there are
beautiful paintings
by V. V. Reiner.

Der Blick zum Wischehrad vom Smíchover Ufer aus läßt die Vorstellung vom alten Sitz der Přemyslidenfürsten und -könige wach werden, hoch wie er auf steilem Felsen über dem Fluß aufragt.
<

Romanische Rotunde des hl. Martin aus der 2. Hälfte des 11. Jh.

View of Vyšehrad from the Smíchov bank of the River Vltava evokes the idea of the ancient seat of the Přemyslid princes and kings, situated on a sheer rock overlooking the water.
<

The Romanesque Rotunda of St. Martin of the latter half of the 11th century.

VYŠEHRAD

Nach der episodenhaften Bedeutsamkeit des Wischehrads unter Vratislav II. in der zweiten Hälfte des 11. Jahrhunderts blieb seine Position in der Folgezeit zweitrangig. Erst Karl IV. ließ die Burg erneut befestigen und errichtete 1364 an der Stelle der Vratislawschen Basilika eine gotische Kapitelkirche und betonte die Bedeutung dieses Ortes auch dadurch, daß hier der Krönungszug seinen Anfang nahm.

VYŠEHRAD

After the episodical growth of the importance of Vyšehrad during the reign of Vratislav II in the latter half of the 11th century the Přemyslid seat stagnated in a second-rank position until the time of Charles IV, who had the castle newly fortified and, after 1364, a Gothic chapter church built on the site of Vratislav's basilica. He also stressed the importance of the locality by having the coronation procession begin here.

Pseudoromanisches Portal, Ende 19. Jh. Es führt zu den Ausgrabungen der romanischen Basilika des hl. Laurenzius, der dritten Kirche, die durch Vratislav II. auf dem Wischehrad gegründet worden war.

>
Blick von Osten auf die Kapitelkirche St. Peter und Paul in pseudogotischem Stil, den J. Mocker durch Umbauten von 1885-99 prägte.

A pseudo-Romanesque portal of the late 19th century leads to the excavations of the Romanesque Basilica of St. Lawrence, the third church founded on Vyšehrad by Vratislav II.

>
View from the east of the chapter church consecrated to SS. Peter and Paul in the pseudo-Gothic form lent its main features by the modifications carried out by J. Mocker from 1885 to 1899.

VYŠEHRAD

Ende 1420, nach dem Sieg der Hussiten über die Truppen Kaisers Siegmund bemächtigten sich die Prager den Wischehrad, bald wurde er besiedelt und zur Stadt erhoben. Nach 1654 wurde er in eine barocke Festung umgewandelt, in der das Kapitel erhalten blieb. In der zweiten Hälfte des 19. Jahrhunderts wurde hier die nationale Begräbnisstätte eingerichtet.

VYŠEHRAD

After the victory of the Hussites over the troops of the Emperor Sigismund at the end of 1420 the citizens of Prague demolished Vyšehrad. Later it was settled and raised to a town. After 1654 it was converted into a Baroque fortress in which the chapter has been preserved. The national cemetery was established here in the latter half of the 19th century.

ST. MARGARETA

Die Benediktinerkirche zur hl. Margareta wurde durch Boleslav II. im Dorf Břevnov westlich der Prager Burg gegründet. Aus ihren Anfängen erhielt sich die Krypta aus dem 11. Jahrhundert, die an die ursprüngliche Konventkirche des hl. Adalbert angrenzt. Das heutige Kloster errichtete 1709–16 K. Dientzenhofer unter Beteiligung seines Sohnes Kilian Ignaz. Das monumentale Äußere der Kirche entspricht auch seinem Inneren, das einheitlich und gleichzeitig durch seine gewellt-gekrümmten Wände dynamisch wirkt.

ST. MARGARET'S CHURCH

The Benedictine Church of St. Margaret was founded by Boleslav II in the village of Břevnov lying to the west of Prague Castle. The 11th century crypt belonging to the original convent Church of St. Adalbert has been preserved of its oldest form. The present monastery was built in the years 1709 to 1716 by Kryštof Dientzenhofer with the participation of his son Kilián Ignác. The monumental exterior of the church is matched by its interior whose compact and simultaneously dynamic effect is created by the undulating curves of its walls.

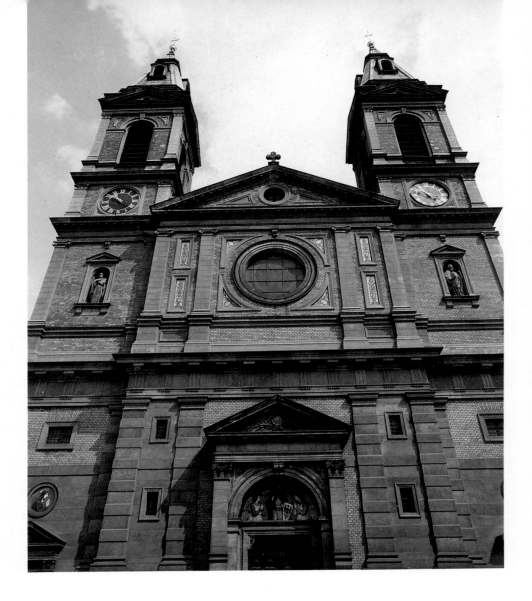

ST. WENZEL

Smíchov, bis zu Beginn des 19. Jahrhunderts
eine bukolische Landschaft der Gärten,
Weingärten und einzelner adliger und
bürgerlicher Sommerfrischler, entwickelte sich
rasch zu einer Industrievorstadt, seit 1848
Selbstverwaltung, 1920 mit Prag verschmolzen.
Die Bedeutung und das Selbstbewußtsein
der Smíchov-Bewohner spiegelt sich im Bau der
erzbischöflichen St.-Wenzels-Kirche, einer
Basilika im Stile der Neurenaissance aus den
Jahren 1881-85.

ST. WENCESLAS'S CHURCH

Smíchov, until the early 19th century
a bucolic region of gardens, vineyards
and small homesteads of the nobility and
burghers, rapidly became an industrial suburb.
From 1848 it was an autonomous town and
in 1920 it became a part of Prague.
The importance and self-confidence
of the burghers of Smíchov were reflected
in the form of the archidecanal Church
of St. Wenceslas, a Neo-Renaissance basilica
built between in 1881 and 1885.

ST. LUDMILLA

Ähnlich wie Smíchov entstand auch das Stadtgebiet Königliche Weinberge in einem Streifen Grün entlang der neustädtischen Wälle, im Grunde allerdings als Wohnviertel mit überwiegendem Anteil an Mietshäusern. Nach der Zuerkennung der Stadtrechte im Jahre 1879 entschied man sich bald für die Errichtung der der hl. Ludmilla geweihten Kirche. Der dreischiffige neugotische Ziegelbau der Kirche wurde in den Jahren 1888–93 durch Josef Mocker errichtet. Das Tympanon des Portals stammt von J. V. Myslbek.

ST. LUDMILA'S CHURCH

Similarly as Smíchov, Vinohrady also originated in a zone of greenery running along the fortifications of the New Town. In essence, however, it had the character of a residential quarter mainly filled with apartment houses. Soon after the raising of Vinohrady to a town the construction of an archidecanal church consecrated to St. Ludmila was started. This triple-naved, Neo-Gothic brick-built basilica was erected from 1888 to 1893 by Josef Mocker. The tympanum on the main portal was sculptured by J. V. Myslbek.

ST. WENZEL

Nach dem ersten Weltkrieg setzte sich in Prag schrittweise die Avantgarde der Architektur durch, vor allem in Bauten von Wohn-, Verwaltungs- und Produktionsprojekten. In der Mitte der Zwischenkriegszeit kam es auch zur Realisierung einiger Sakralbauten. Dazu zählt auch ein Werk des Architekten J. Gočár, die St.-Wenzel-Kirche aus den Jahren 1929–30 mit ihrer Innenausstattung durch zeitgenössische tschechische Künstler.

ST. WENCESLAS'S CHURCH

After the First World War the architectural avant-garde asserted itself gradually, chiefly in residential, administrative and industrial buildings. Midway between the two world wars several sacral buildings were also erected, their number including architect Josef Gočár's St. Wenceslas's Church (1929–1930) with interior decoration by contemporary Czech artists.

HERZ-JESU-KIRCHE
Die Persönlichkeit des slowenischen Architekten
Josif Plecnik kam vor allem bei Rekonstruktionsarbeiten
der Prager Burg in der Zeit nach dem ersten Weltkrieg
und in seiner pädagogischen Tätigkeit zum Tragen.
Die einzige Realisierung eines Plecnik-Projektes
haben wir in der Pfarrkirche Herz Jesu auf dem Platz
Georg von Poděbrad im Stadtviertel Königliche
Weinberge vor uns. Plecnik ließ hier seiner Vorliebe
für antiquierende Dispositionen und Formensprache
freien Lauf. Die Kirche wurde 1928–30 errichtet.

THE CHURCH OF THE HEART OF JESUS
The personality of the Slovenian architect
Josif Plecnik manifested itself mainly in modifications
of Prague Castle in the period after the First World
War and in his pedagogical work. A unique realization
of one of Plecnik's projects is the parish Church
of the Heart of Jesus in Jiří z Poděbrad Square
in Vinohrady. In this work the architect applied his
bent for a Neo-Classical ground-plan and conception
of forms. The church was built from
1928 to 1930.

Register

Jungfrau Maria-St. Elisabethkloster
Our Lady – St. Elisabeth's Convent

St. Simeon und Juda
SS. Simeon and Judah

St. Maria Magdalena
St. Mary Magdalen's

St. Johann Nepomuk-Hradčany
St. John Nepomuk's-Hradčany

Jubiläumssynagoge
Jubilee Synagogue

St. Martin in der Mauer
St. Martin's in the Wall

St. Michael
St. Michael's

Hl. Kreuz (Piaristen)
Holy Rood (Piarist Convent)

St. Rochus
St. Rochus's

Index

St. Adalbert
St. Adalbert's

St. Klemens
St. Clement's

St. Laurentius
St. Lawrence's

Dreifaltigkeitskirche
Holy Trinity

Marienkirche „Na Slupi"
Our Lady "Na Slupi"

St. Michael
St. Michael's

St. Pancratius
St. Pancratius's

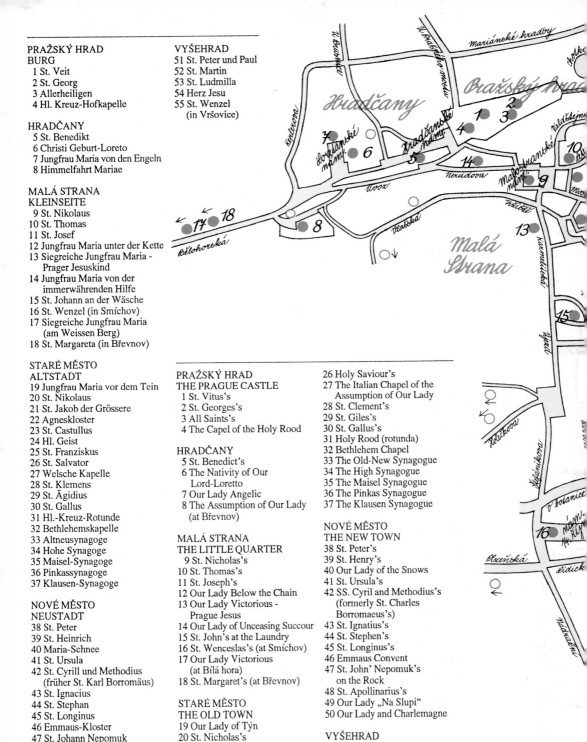

PRAŽSKÝ HRAD
BURG
1 St. Veit
2 St. Georg
3 Allerheiligen
4 Hl. Kreuz-Hofkapelle

HRADČANY
5 St. Benedikt
6 Christi Geburt-Loreto
7 Jungfrau Maria von den Engeln
8 Himmelfahrt Mariae

MALÁ STRANA
KLEINSEITE
9 St. Nikolaus
10 St. Thomas
11 St. Josef
12 Jungfrau Maria unter der Kette
13 Siegreiche Jungfrau Maria -
   Prager Jesuskind
14 Jungfrau Maria von der
   immerwährenden Hilfe
15 St. Johann an der Wäsche
16 St. Wenzel (in Smíchov)
17 Siegreiche Jungfrau Maria
   (am Weissen Berg)
18 St. Margareta (in Břevnov)

STARÉ MĚSTO
ALTSTADT
19 Jungfrau Maria vor dem Tein
20 St. Nikolaus
21 St. Jakob der Grössere
22 Agneskloster
23 St. Castullus
24 Hl. Geist
25 St. Franziskus
26 St. Salvator
27 Welsche Kapelle
28 St. Klemens
29 St. Ägidius
30 St. Gallus
31 Hl.-Kreuz-Rotunde
32 Bethlehemskapelle
33 Altneusynagoge
34 Hohe Synagoge
35 Maisel-Synagoge
36 Pinkassynagoge
37 Klausen-Synagoge

NOVÉ MĚSTO
NEUSTADT
38 St. Peter
39 St. Heinrich
40 Maria-Schnee
41 St. Ursula
42 St. Cyrill und Methodius
   (früher St. Karl Borromäus)
43 St. Ignacius
44 St. Stephan
45 St. Longinus
46 Emmaus-Kloster
47 St. Johann Nepomuk
   am Felsen
48 St. Apollinarius
49 Marienkirche „Na Slupi"
50 Jungfrau Maria und Karl
   der Große

VYŠEHRAD
51 St. Peter und Paul
52 St. Martin
53 St. Ludmilla
54 Herz Jesu
55 St. Wenzel
   (in Vršovice)

PRAŽSKÝ HRAD
THE PRAGUE CASTLE
1 St. Vitus's
2 St. Georges's
3 All Saints's
4 The Capel of the Holy Rood

HRADČANY
5 St. Benedict's
6 The Nativity of Our
   Lord-Loretto
7 Our Lady Angelic
8 The Assumption of Our Lady
   (at Břevnov)

MALÁ STRANA
THE LITTLE QUARTER
9 St. Nicholas's
10 St. Thomas's
11 St. Joseph's
12 Our Lady Below the Chain
13 Our Lady Victorious -
   Prague Jesus
14 Our Lady of Unceasing Succour
15 St. John's at the Laundry
16 St. Wenceslas's (at Smíchov)
17 Our Lady Victorious
   (at Bílá hora)
18 St. Margaret's (at Břevnov)

STARÉ MĚSTO
THE OLD TOWN
19 Our Lady of Týn
20 St. Nicholas's
21 St. James the Greater's
22 The Convent of St. Agnes
23 St. Castullus's
24 The Holy Spirit
25 St. Francis's of Assisi

26 Holy Saviour's
27 The Italian Chapel of the
   Assumption of Our Lady
28 St. Clement's
29 St. Giles's
30 St. Gallus's
31 Holy Rood (rotunda)
32 Bethlehem Chapel
33 The Old-New Synagogue
34 The High Synagogue
35 The Maisel Synagogue
36 The Pinkas Synagogue
37 The Klausen Synagogue

NOVÉ MĚSTO
THE NEW TOWN
38 St. Peter's
39 St. Henry's
40 Our Lady of the Snows
41 St. Ursula's
42 SS. Cyril and Methodius's
   (formerly St. Charles
   Borromaeus's)
43 St. Ignatius's
44 St. Stephen's
45 St. Longinus's
46 Emmaus Convent
47 St. John' Nepomuk's
   on the Rock
48 St. Apollinarius's
49 Our Lady „Na Slupi"
50 Our Lady and Charlemagne

VYŠEHRAD
51 SS. Peter and Paul
52 St. Martin's
53 St. Ludmila's
54 Heart of Jesus
55 St. Wenceslas's (at Vršovice)